D0457320

DISCARD

Diseases and Disorders

Learning Disabilities

Titles in the Diseases and Disorders series include:

Diseases and Disorders

Learning
Disabilities

by Christina M. Girod

Library of Congress Cataloging-in-Publication Data

Girod, Christina M.
    Learning disabilities / by Christina Girod.
        p. cm. — (Diseases and disorders)
    Discusses what a learning disability is, types of learning disorders, growing up with a learning disorder, diagnosis and intervention, adults coping with learning disorders, and current trends in research and education.
    Includes bibliographical references (p.) and index.
    ISBN 1-56006-844-2 (lib.: alk. paper)
    1. Learning disabilities—Juvenile literature. 2. Learning disabled—Education—Juvenile literature. [1. Learning disabilities.]
    I. Title. II. Diseases and disorders series.
    LC4704.G57   2001
    371.9—dc21   00-011290

Table of Contents

"The Most Difficult Puzzles Ever Devised"

CHARLES BEST, ONE of the pioneers in the search for a cure for diabetes, once explained what it is about medical research that intrigued him so. "It's not just the gratification of knowing one is helping people," he confided, "although that probably is a more heroic and selfless motivation. Those feelings may enter in, but truly, what I find best is the feeling of going toe to toe with nature, of trying to solve the most difficult puzzles ever devised. The answers are there somewhere, those keys that will solve the puzzle and make the patient well. But how will those keys be found?"

Since the dawn of civilization, nothing has so puzzled people—and often frightened them, as well—as the onset of illness in a body or mind that had seemed healthy before. A seizure, the inability of a heart to pump, the sudden deterioration of muscle tone in a small child—being unable to reverse such conditions or even to understand why they occur was unspeakably frustrating to healers. Even before there were names for such conditions, even before they were understood at all, each was a reminder of how complex the human body was, and how vulnerable.

While our grappling with understanding diseases has been frustrating at times, it has also provided some of humankind's most heroic accomplishments. Alexander Fleming's accidental discovery in 1928 of a mold that could be turned into penicillin has resulted in the saving of untold millions of lives. The isolation of the enzyme insulin has reversed what was once a death sentence for anyone with diabetes. There have been great strides in combating conditions for which there is not yet a cure, too. Medicines can help AIDS patients live longer, diagnostic tools such as mammography and ultrasounds can help doctors find tumors while they are treatable, and laser surgery techniques have made the most intricate, minute operations routine.

This "toe-to-toe" competition with diseases and disorders is even more remarkable when seen in a historical continuum. An astonishing amount of progress has been made in a very short time. Just two hundred years ago, the existence of germs as a cause of some diseases was unknown. In fact, it was less than 150 years ago that a British surgeon named Joseph Lister had difficulty persuading his fellow doctors that washing their hands before delivering a baby might increase the chances of a healthy delivery (especially if they had just attended to a diseased patient)!

Each book in Lucent's *Diseases and Disorders* series explores a disease or disorder and the knowledge that has been accumulated (or discarded) by doctors through the years. Each book also examines the tools used for pinpointing a diagnosis, as well as the various means that are used to treat or cure a disease. Finally, new ideas are presented—techniques or medicines that may be on the horizon.

Frustration and disappointment are still part of medicine, for not every disease or condition can be cured or prevented. But the limitations of knowledge are being pushed outward constantly; the "most difficult puzzles ever devised" are finding challengers every day.

Introduction

I'M IN THE sixth grade now and am doing OK, I think. I'm the lucky one of the family for two of my three older brothers had a pretty rough time in school. . . . I can remember when I was little I used to say to my folks, "I hear you but I don't understand you." Even now, I have to listen "hard" in school. . . . I used to always say "I'm stupid." Seems like I just couldn't get along with the kids either. They used to call me dumb lots of times. . . . I can still remember way back in the first grade when I used to "scrub" my pencil across the paper. Sometimes I did it all day; I just couldn't do anything the other kids did and that really made me mad. I couldn't read either. In the second grade I started getting lots of extra help. I began to find I really could learn but it just took a lot longer for me. I had a very special kind of help in reading.[1]

This is the story of Bobby, a twelve-year-old with a learning disability. He could not write or even tell his story in a way others would understand, so someone had to help him find the words to express himself. Bobby and his brothers' lives are complicated by their learning disabilities. Some everyday tasks—driving, chatting with friends, dialing a phone number, reading a book, or writing a letter—can be daily struggles for someone with a learning disability.

The Definition of a Learning Disability

Today it is generally agreed that a learning disability is the inability of an individual of average or above-average intelligence to achieve success in school or work. Learning disabilities are usually neurological in origin, and they impede a person's ability to process, store, or produce information, which prevents a person from achieving personal, academic, and professional goals. These disorders are specific to the individual and affect a person throughout life. The National Joint Committee on Learning Disabilities states

The simple act of reading a book can be a difficult endeavor for a child with a learning disability.

that problems with social skills and managing time and space may exist with learning disabilities, but they are not by themselves learning disabilities.

Who Has a Learning Disability?

About 5 percent of the U.S. population, or over 12 million people, have learning disabilities. The U.S. Department of Education estimates that half of all students receiving special-education services in the public schools, which constitutes about 5 percent of the total student population, are identified as learning disabled.

It is important to understand the nature of learning disabilities because they affect a large portion of the population, and many of these people are not diagnosed. The greater the understanding that society has of learning disabilities, the more likely those who have them will lead productive lives. Although this effort was only begun in the last few decades, educational and medical researchers are discovering new information that can help people with learning disabilities accomplish their goals.

Chapter 1

History and Types of Learning Disabilities

THE HISTORY OF learning disabilities is only about a century old, and at first it referred only to reading problems. Throughout the twentieth century, as scientists discovered more about how the human brain works, the term *learning disabilities* came to mean much more. Today there are four recognized types of learning disabilities. However, because many of their symptoms overlap, it is sometimes difficult to distinguish between them. This confusion has caused disagreement between professionals about the proper definition of a learning disability.

Early History of Learning Disabilities

The idea of a learning disability dates back to the work of two physicians, Samuel Orton and James Hinshelwood, who were the first to notice that some people have similar learning problems. In the early 1900s several parents took their children to Orton and Hinshelwood to be evaluated because the children were experiencing trouble learning to read. Though they found no physical causes, the two physicians did notice that many of these children showed similar types of behavior when they tried to read. For instance, the children would often reverse the order of letters in a word, such as reading *tab* when the word was actually *bat*. They documented these difficulties, noting that these children could not read even though they received formal instruction, came from average socioeconomic backgrounds, and otherwise possessed average or above-average intelligence.

In 1917 Hinshelwood published his observations of a thirteen-year-old boy who could remember information he heard but could not recall visual symbols such as letters and numbers. He speculated that the boy's difficulties stemmed from a neurological problem. Hinshelwood called this learning difficulty "word blindness." Orton, on the other hand, who also published observations of word blindness, believed the difficulties were caused by a lack of cerebral dominance (in most people, either the left or the right side of the brain is dominant). He believed equal control between the two sides of the brain resulted in abnormal brain wiring, which sent visual information from the eye to the wrong part of the brain. Studies of neurological problems in people with reading difficulties continued through the 1920s and 1930s until another researcher approached the problem differently.

In the 1930s a psychologist named Mable Fernald studied the psychological characteristics of children who had problems learning to read. She was one of the first professionals to speculate that such reading difficulties might be rooted in differences in how these children's brains processed information. She thought that if the way they were being taught was changed, maybe they *could* learn. Fernald noticed that although most children learn to read despite different teaching methods, children who had problems learning to read did not. She was one of the first to develop a method of teaching such children to read, called Visual, Auditory, Kinesthetic, and Tactile (VAKT). Fernald's VAKT method required using all of the senses when learning to read. Children were given opportunities to see (look at the printed word *cat* on paper), hear (listen to someone say the word *cat),* touch (trace the letters of the word *cat* in flour or on letters cut from sandpaper), smell (sniff different things that start with the letter *f,* such as fudge, flowers, or fish), taste (taste different things that start with the letter *c,* such as cake, candy, or carrots), and manipulate letters and words (make letters or words out of clay). This is called a multisensory approach, and today it is a highly recommended method for teaching all academic subjects to children who have learning disabilities.

A preschooler learns the alphabet by tracing letters. This form of teaching assists students afflicted by visual-perceptual learning disabilities.

Difficulty Acquiring a Definition

Although for decades reading problems were the focus of learning disabilities, by the 1960s researchers and educators had expanded this realm to include problems with math, speech, and writing. In 1963 Samuel Kirk, a mental-health professional and special-education pioneer, used the term *learning disabilities* for the first time while speaking to a group of parents, educators, and professionals who later formed the Association of Children with Learning Disabilities. During his speech, Kirk stated, "Recently, I have used the term 'learning disabilities' to describe a group of children who have disorders in development in language, speech, reading, and associated communication skills needed for social interactions."[2]

To identify students who had learning disabilities, however, an official and standard definition of the term *learning disability* needed to be adopted. Since the 1960s, educators, professionals, and lawmakers have disagreed about the definition of the term. Many do not think the definition provided by the National Joint Committee on Learning Disabilities is general enough, and they disagree with the exclusion of social difficulties and self-regulatory behaviors. In addition, learning disabilities are sometimes complicated by the presence of another disability, such as a hearing loss or an attention deficit disorder. Although learning disabilities may occur with other disabilities (for example, vision or hearing loss, mental retardation, or serious emotional problems) or with outside influences (such as cultural differences or poor teaching), they are not the result of these other disabilities or influences.

Much of the problem lies in the fact that learning disabilities encompass a broad range of disorders, including difficulties in reading, spelling, writing, mathematics, spoken language, socialization, and other areas. Moreover, the level of severity differs in each case. These differences make forming a standard profile for students who have learning disabilities impossible. The possible combinations are endless; for instance, one child with a learning disability may read well but understand little of what is read, another child may read below grade average but remembers everything that is heard, and a third child may read

A child with a learning disability may read very well but have a difficult time understanding what he reads.

well but cannot write a sentence. Corinne Smith, author and associate dean of education at Syracuse University, and Lisa Strick, a freelance writer, explain why the term *learning disability* is so difficult to define:

> Learning disabilities . . . often occur in combinations—and also vary tremendously in severity—it can be very hard to see what students grouped under this label have in common. In fact, learning disabilities are often so subtle that these children do not seem handicapped at all. Many children with learning disabilities have intelligences in the average to superior range, and what is usually most obvious about them is that they are able (even exceptionally so) in some areas.[3]

Although a legal definition was first developed in 1975, it has changed over time as professionals have tried to create a more comprehensive definition. The challenge has been to create a definition that encompasses all of the behaviors associated with learning disabilities yet is narrow enough to exclude those disorders or conditions that are not learning disabilities.

Causes of Learning Disabilities

Despite disagreement about how to define *learning disabilities,* most researchers agree that such disabilities are often hereditary, meaning that they have a genetic cause. Scientists have identified four chromosomes that may carry the genetic information related to learning disabilities. Chromosomes are structures in human cells that hold the genes, the basic units of heredity that hand down traits from parents to children. Genes control how a person develops from a single cell into a human being. Parents may pass genetic information to their children that causes the brain to process information differently than most people do. In one study, 60 percent of children with learning disabilities had family members who also had similar disabilities, and another study showed that 88 percent had relatives with learning disabilities. After evaluating a child's family history, a learning disability can often be attributed to a genetic cause, as one learning-disability specialist discovered with one of her students, Jimmy:

When Jimmy's mother called the clinic to refer her son for an evaluation, the first hint that Jimmy's learning difficulties might be hereditary came over the phone. Jimmy's mother expressed her deep "flustration" in obtaining adequate services for her son's "dilekia." From a woman with a Ph.D. who was the director of a counseling center, such mispronunciations were unexpected. The mother's worst fear was that Jimmy had inherited "dilekia" from both sides of the family. Jimmy's mother had two siblings, neither of whom had learned to read until adolescence. One now writes books, but remains a terrible speller. One child of the other sibling has been identified as learning disabled. . . . Jimmy's father was very late in learning to read and still reads, in his words, "a word an hour." What he reads he remembers, however. . . . Jimmy's father comes from a family of five children, and every one has a reading disability.[4]

Researchers believe the gene causes a difference in brain "wiring" or variations in the size of some areas of the brain, resulting in a learning disability. Anatomical studies have shown that electrical activity in the area of the brain known as V5/MT, which is the area responsible for movement, perception, and the language-processing parts of the brains, of learning-disabled individuals differs from the brains of nondisabled persons. Guinevere Eden, a scientist at the National Institute of Mental Health, says, "We found that maps of brain activity measured while subjects were given a visual task of looking at moving dots were very different in individuals with dyslexia [a type of learning disability] compared to normal control subjects."[5] The control subjects showed intense activity in the V5/MT brain area while viewing the moving dots. However, there was almost no activity in this area of the brain in the dyslexic subjects.

Scientists speculate that different sizes or locations of brain areas may cause neural pathways (brain wiring) to follow different directions than they would in most people's brains. Thus, information obtained through the eyes or the ears follows a neural pathway that does not carry it to the appropriate brain location that processes this type of information. Scientists are not certain whether the information goes to the wrong part of the brain or if

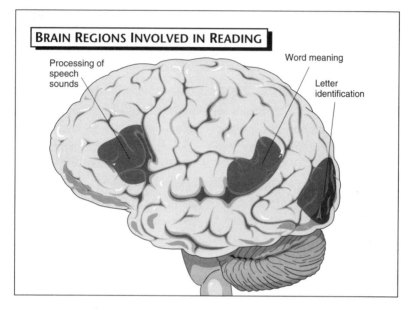

BRAIN REGIONS INVOLVED IN READING

Processing of speech sounds

Word meaning

Letter identification

it arrives in the correct area but is jumbled along the pathway. This deviation can be manifested, for example, as dyslexia, the learning disability characterized by a variation in the brain wiring that connects visual information (such as letters or numerals) to the part of the brain that turns it into auditory language (such as the sounds of the letters or names of the numerals).

Learning disabilities caused by brain injury are less common than those caused by genetics. Accidents that cause head trauma, such as an automobile crash, a near drowning, or choking, can sometimes cause brain damage that creates gaps in the neurological wiring. Complications during birth or prematurity can result in similar brain damage. Usually the damage stems from either a lack of oxygen to the baby during labor and delivery or to underdeveloped lungs or heart problems in premature infants. Severe illnesses, such as meningitis, malnutrition, and exposure to toxins like lead poisoning, also may cause missing neurological links that disrupt normal brain activity. This disruption may result in a learning disability, as it did in the case of two-year-old David.

Shortly after his second birthday, David had begun to speak in sentences and to use a vocabulary of about five hundred words. He was an extremely verbal and outgoing child. A couple of months later, David suffered an allergic reaction after receiving an immunization shot. He had several seizures, and during one he stopped breathing for about sixty seconds. David survived, but the seizure had caused damage to the language-processing areas of his brain. Six months after the incident he was unable to speak in sentences, and his vocabulary decreased to two hundred words. Years later, his problems with language processing made reading comprehension and written expression difficult for him.

Regardless of the cause—whether genetic or a brain injury—the problem always begins in the neural pathways of the brain and manifests itself in one or more of the four types of learning disabilities.

General Types of Learning Disabilities

Learning disabilities can be divided into four major types. Within each type are several specific learning disabilities, which are defined by certain behaviors. Both children and adults may exhibit any of these types of learning disabilities. However, most researchers and professionals focus on learning disabilities in public schools because it is easier to examine these different types by observing school-age children.

Fine-Motor Disabilities

Some people have problems with fine-motor skills, which is the ability to do various things with the hands, such as writing and holding or gripping an object. It takes fine-motor skills to eat with a spoon and fork, to cut with scissors, and to pour juice from a pitcher into a cup. People who have fine-motor disabilities find these activities a challenge, one that impacts their school performance. To someone with a fine-motor disability, writing is like trying to print a word on a piece of paper while looking at the image in a mirror. The mirror image confuses the brain, which cannot guide the hand to correctly form the letters and in turn causes poor handwriting.

Poor handwriting is characterized by illegible writing, inconsistent spacing and letter size, and an inability to stay on a line. Writing is often such difficult work for a student with a fine-motor disability that completing written assignments on time is challenging. The content and organization of written work often suffers because nearly all of the effort is directed toward achieving legibility. In math, numbers are often copied illegibly and poorly aligned, resulting in incorrect computations.

Art is frequently a difficult task for students with fine-motor disabilities. Their work is looked upon as sloppy because of problems with holding and controlling pencils, crayons, markers, glue, and scissors. They often cannot color within the lines, and drawings are unrecognizable or immature for their age. In addition, they cannot cut on a line or control the amount of glue squeezed from the bottle.

Children with fine-motor problems also appear clumsy or awkward because they frequently drop and spill things and knock things over. Picking up and using small items, such as puzzle pieces, Legos, or blocks, is frustrating. Self-dressing, which involves buttoning, zipping, snapping, hooking, buckling, and tying, is often a laborious daily chore. Alexander's experiences in the fourth grade, recounted by a learning-disability specialist, indicate a fine-motor disability:

> Testing showed that Alexander was an incredibly gifted child.
> His vocabulary and reasoning ability were equal to those of
> most adults. He scored at high school level in all areas of

Cutting a straight line with scissors may be a struggle for a youngster with a fine-motor disability.

achievement with the exception of written expression, where his achievement was average for his age and grade. Alexander's spelling, sentence structure, and punctuation were perfect, but he took an unduly long time getting words down on paper. . . . Alexander's writing difficulties were found to be primarily due to very poor motor planning. He could not write a word without actually thinking about telling his hand how to move. It was also difficult for him to touch his thumb to each successive finger, figure out how to skip, or walk through a doorway without bumping into the frame. [He] often dropped tableware when setting the table, and . . . getting a coin into a vending machine slot was very difficult for him.[6]

Dyspraxia, a type of fine-motor disability, affects the ability to coordinate purposeful body movements, such as Alexander's problems with writing. Dyspraxia is unusual in that it can also affect speech movements, resulting in problems sending a message from the brain to the mouth. For example, Joe has no problem understanding what others say to him or thinking about what he wants to say. However, his dyspraxia prevents him from saying it. Joe recalls how his disability affected him at school: "If a teacher were to ask me what county I lived in, I could be thinking 'Gallatin County' and out would pop 'America.' This would happen often. . . . There were times I would . . . say something and my friends would look at me like I was from another planet."[7] Joe was unable to make his mouth form the appropriate words for what he was thinking.

Nonverbal Learning Disabilities

Nonverbal disabilities primarily include problems with reasoning, which affects organization and visual discrimination. This is due to logical thought being distorted along the pathway to or in the reasoning area of the brain.

Although students with nonverbal disabilities read fluently and remember the facts of the story, they mix up the sequence of events and fail to grasp cause-and-effect relationships. For example, Joey, a kindergartner with a nonverbal disability, is a quick

Speech therapists are often employed to help kids overcome dyspraxia, a fine-motor disability which affects normal speaking.

reader and is in the highest level primer in his class. After reading *Goldilocks and the Three Bears,* he remembers all of the characters in the story, where it took place, and that it involved bowls of porridge, a broken chair, and three beds. However, Joey cannot remember if Goldilocks broke the chair before or after she tasted the porridge. Furthermore, he does not understand what caused Goldilocks to run away from the house at the end of the story (the bears scared her).

In math and science, students with nonverbal disabilities easily master facts such as multiplication tables, geometry theorems, and the periodic table of elements. However, they encounter difficulty with reasoning skills necessary in understanding chemistry. For instance, a student with a nonverbal disability may have difficulty understanding how certain chemical substances combine to create an explosion because he or she lacks the reasoning abilities to grasp the cause-and-effect relationship between the substances.

Nonverbal disabilities affect other skills that require reasoning abilities. Artwork, such as drawing a house to scale, can be difficult to achieve because the student must be able to take information on the depth, length, and width of the house in relation to all of its parts and reasonably devise the correct angles for the walls, doors, and windows. Moreover, nonverbal disabilities make interpretation of social cues, like facial expressions, body language, and emotions, a challenge. The failure to understand cause-and-effect relationships makes it difficult to anticipate the consequences of one's actions.

Visual-Perceptual Disabilities

Visual perception is the ability to recognize and interpret what is seen through the eyes. For example, a child who learns to recognize the letter-symbol *B* and its associated sound is demonstrating visual-perceptual skills. Children who have problems with visual perception have difficulty in making sense out of what they see. This is due to a problem with how their brains process visual information, not with how well their eyes function. Normally, a visual picture travels along the nerve path from the eyes to the brain's visual cortex to deliver an image. However, in a learning-disabled individual the picture is distorted because of a variation in how the image is delivered or in how the visual cortex interprets it. Visual-perceptual disabilities cause problems with recognizing and understanding letters, words, numbers, math symbols, diagrams, maps, charts, and graphs.

Finding the North Pole on a globe is not too difficult for a child with a visual-perception problem; remembering its location a week later is the real challenge.

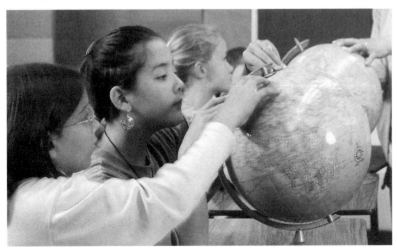

Students who have visual-perceptual disabilities exhibit problems with writing, reading, mathematics, and organizational skills. Difficulties in writing are apparent by messy and incomplete papers with a great deal of erasing and crossing out, frequent letter and number reversals, uneven spacing between letters and words, problems copying other printed materials, poor spelling, and trouble organizing written work.

Visual-perceptual problems in reading result in confusing similar letters (such as *b* for *d* or *p* for *q*), confusing similar words (such as *beard* and *bread*), reversing words (reading *was* for *saw*), difficulty finding letters within words or words within sentences (cannot point out the *r* while sounding out the word *trap*), and problems remembering "sight words" (such as *the* or *and*). Reading difficulties also include losing one's place in reading and poor comprehension of main ideas.

Students who have visual-perceptual disabilities experience difficulties in mathematics as well. They may have trouble understanding higher-level math concepts and with remembering math facts, multiplication tables, formulas, and equations. They frequently misalign math problems, resulting in computational errors.

Problems with organization and perception are also symptoms of a visual-perceptual disability. Students confuse left and right, often lose things, and have a poor sense of direction. They also have problems with being on time and judging speed and distance. Puzzles and mazes can be very difficult for those with visual-perceptual disabilities. Socially, they have trouble getting to the point in conversations, and they do not easily interpret others' moods or visual cues.

Most of the time visual-perceptual disabilities are not obvious until a child reaches first grade, when the curriculum is overflowing with visual information that the child must learn, including letters, sight words (such as *the, at,* or *and*), numbers, and simple math symbols. One mother recounts the visual-perceptual difficulties her son had in first grade:

> Seth learned to talk early, and by five he had a near adult vocabulary. He was relentlessly curious and loved being read to.

If this boy has trouble writing on the board, he may suffer from a language-processing disability such as dysphasia.

. . . He couldn't wait to start school. . . . Seth loved kindergarten, but his attitude toward school changed completely in first grade. . . . By the end of October he was saying he hated school and didn't want to go anymore. . . . [Seth's teacher said] he was falling behind in every subject. He couldn't keep up with even the slowest group in reading. . . . The teacher gave me flash cards for thirty sight words she wanted Seth to learn so he could get started in the first-grade reading primer. I chose three to start with. . . . We drilled those words for a week. . . . At the end of the week, Seth couldn't recognize a single word. He didn't recognize any at the end of the second week either. . . . He also started saying he didn't want me to read to him any more. . . . Finally . . . I asked the school to test Seth for anything they could think of that might be contributing to all these problems. By the end of the semester we had an explanation: Seth had a gifted IQ and a learning disability. His main problem was visual memory; he understood things just fine when he was looking at them, but he couldn't seem to hold onto any kind of mental picture.[8]

Language-Processing Disabilities

The most common group of learning disabilities involves language processing, which affects both written and spoken communication. Language-processing disabilities are character-ized by difficulties hearing words correctly, understanding word meanings, and remembering verbal material. This is due to a problem with how the brain processes language. Usually, lan-guage information travels along the nerve path from the ears or the eyes to the language areas of the brain. However, in a learning-disabled individual the words, letters, sentences, or other language information is distorted because of a variation in how it is deliv-ered or in how the brain interprets it. Unlike visual-perceptual problems, language disabilities are often evident at an earlier age, when a child is learning to talk. Early problems may include learn-ing to talk at a slower rate, speaking in shorter sentences, using smaller vocabularies, and using more immature grammar than most other children of the same age.

By the time a child begins school, other indications of a language-processing disability may appear. Such behavior includes often confusing words that have similar sounds (such as *borrow* and *to-morrow*, or forming a new word like *bomorrow*), insensitivity to rhyming (given three words—*fat*, *cat*, and *sit*—cannot recognize fat and cat as rhyming words), giving inappropriate answers to questions (such as replying "Spaghetti" to the question "Do you buy your lunch at school?"), and an inability to remember or un-derstand instructions.

Language-processing disabilities affect reading in a variety of ways. A student may have difficulty naming letters and learning their sounds, discriminating between sounds in words, and blending sounds into words. Letters within a word are mixed up, such as reading *snug* for *sung*. Reading is very slow and compre-hension is poor.

Writing is equally affected by language disabilities. Written work is usually brief or incomplete, the vocabulary limited, and the grammar and spelling poor. In addition, ideas are not clearly organized or well developed.

In mathematics, a language-processing disability is evidenced by slow response to fact drills, during which numbers must be retrieved from memory. Word problems are especially difficult because the language-disabled student must struggle with poor

Nonverbal disability can cause a child to labor over simple work assignments.

comprehension skills. Furthermore, analysis and logical reasoning limitations make higher-level math problematic.

Dysphasia is a specific kind of language-processing disability characterized by difficulty in using language to communicate (and it is not the result of physical impairments such as damaged vocal cords). In dysphasia, the inability to use words appropriately or retrieve words from memory may affect both written and spoken language. For instance, Sylvia has difficulty finding the words to name objects, but Trina struggles with putting words together in meaningful ways to form sentences.

Other behaviors exhibited by a person with a language disability include garbling telephone messages, misunderstanding what is said on television or the radio, and not understanding jokes or puns. Likewise, comparing or classifying objects is difficult, as is retelling a story in sequence.

The story of Jason, a young man who grew up with a language-processing disability, exemplifies many of these characteristics:

> Jason always did well at remembering concepts but could never remember names, places, and dates . . . and so forth. [In

elementary school] classmates in the lunchroom would outargue him with more accurate facts, no matter what the topic of conversation. He soon learned to retreat socially. . . . Jason's reading and spelling difficulties have continued into adulthood. He has read one novel in his entire life and never reads the newspaper. . . . When writing, Jason can only catch his misspellings after he finishes each word and inspects whether it "looks right." Number reversals occur continually on his order sheets [for his heating-repair business], but he catches these when the sums don't make sense and the order numbers don't match those in the catalogue.[9]

The most common specific kind of language-processing disability is called dyslexia. It is associated only with written forms of language, including reading and writing. Since reading is a fundamental part of a child's education, this disability has the potential to cause problems in every academic area.

Dyslexia

Educators agree that dyslexia is primarily a reading disability, but the World Federation of Neurology defines the term *dyslexia* as "a disorder manifested by failure to attain the language skills of reading, writing and spelling, despite conventional instruction, adequate intelligence and socio-cultural opportunity."[10] With dyslexia, an individual has difficulty linking a spoken word with its visual form. Words and letters provide a visual image that is supposed to be interpreted by the brain as auditory information—this is how our brains turn the letters *c-a-t* into the spoken form of *cat*. In the brain of a dyslexic individual, this image is distorted, preventing him or her from interpreting the letters *c-a-t* as the spoken word *cat*.

Dyslexic students have problems with letter and word reversals (such as *d* for *b* or *but* for *tub*), have a poor visual memory for language symbols (such as the alphabet), and difficulty with letter-sound discrimination (they cannot identify where the *g* sound is in the word *dog*). They also have problems with word sequencing, fluency, word finding, and reading comprehension. Moreover,

Backwards and transposed letters are characteristic of dyslexic writing.

dyslexic individuals find transferring information that is heard to written form difficult, as is using information that has been read. For example, when Susan, a dyslexic sixth-grader, reads a recipe for making a cake, she encounters numerous problems. After much effort sounding out the words, she begins the process of making the cake batter. However, she finds she is confused by what she has just read. Should she add water or oil, or both? How many eggs did the recipe call for? Does the batter need to be mixed to a smooth or a lumpy consistency? When Susan attempts to reread the recipe, she has difficulty locating the information she needs.

For researchers, knowing how information is distorted in the brain is an important part of understanding how the types of learning disabilities differ because their symptoms are very similar. However, the various symptoms are the only outward sign that may help professionals recognize a person who may have a learning disability, leading to a diagnosis of it.

Chapter 2

Diagnosis of Learning Disabilities in Children

TODAY THERE IS a good chance that if a child has a learning disability, a teacher will start the diagnostic process so that the child can receive the help that he or she needs to improve the chances of success in school. Teachers in many states are being trained to recognize learning disabilities. For example, in California and Colorado prospective teachers must take a class on special education as part of their certification program. Many types of disabilities are taught in the class, including physical, sensory impairments, mental retardation, and learning disabilities. The course helps future teachers identify students who may have special needs, including those whose academic, social, and emotional behaviors are characteristic of a learning disability. Teachers also learn to recognize academic, social, and emotional problems that signal a student may be hiding a disability.

Academic Problems

The first traits most teachers recognize in students who may have learning disabilities are behaviors that create academic problems. Teachers look for problems with concentration, attention, memory, and organization. Learning-disabled children frequently appear clumsy, confused, impulsive, or disoriented, as Andrew, a

28

second-grader, did. His teacher noted that Andrew, who had difficulty in reading, often lost his pencil, misplaced his workbooks, got lost in the hallway during bathroom breaks, frequently ran into the corners of tables, and seemed to always be tripping over his own feet.

When teachers notice that a student is having difficulty remembering or applying a skill that has already been taught, they may consider the possibility that this student has a learning disability. In doing schoolwork, children with learning disabilities may have difficulty thinking clearly, writing legibly, spelling correctly, reading, computing, copying forms, remembering facts, following directions, and putting things in order. Casandra, who grew up with a learning disability, recalls how her mother attempted to help her remember the letters of the alphabet when she was a small child. Casandra's behavior is indicative of what teachers (and parents) should be looking for when a learning disability is suspected:

> I can remember my mother making me wear a letter from the alphabet around my neck to school. I think it was the letter *J*. I knew the letter before I left the house and tried so hard not to forget it all day. . . . I walked all the way to school saying the letter *J* over and over again. But do you know over the course of the day I had forgotten that letter? After school was out I

As more about learning disabilities is discovered, many teachers are being trained to recognize their symptoms.

tried so hard—I mean, I looked at that letter, praying that a voice or something would give me the answer before I got home. . . . [I] hated the fact I couldn't remember what she tried so hard to teach me. I remember crying and being mad at myself because I just couldn't get it.[11]

Social Problems

Social problems often accompany academic problems and may also prompt a teacher to test for a learning disability. Academic failure can make children who are learning disabled the target of ridicule among their peers. Sometimes classmates will ostracize children who have learning difficulties, labeling them with hurtful names. "I was a victim of name calling," one adult said of his childhood. "I was called *retard, spaz, SpEd, Mr. Weirdo, dork* all through school."[12] In some cases, children who have language disabilities sometimes have trouble finding the right words when speaking with others. In conversations, Julie got stuck even on simple words and could not speak a sentence fluently. Her peers made fun of her speech and called her names like "Slowpoke." Furthermore, they did not want to play with her or talk to her because they did not want to be associated with Julie's speaking problems.

Teachers need to be aware of how students interact with their peers in the classroom and on the playground. Studies show that learning-disabled students have trouble making and keeping friends. This is due in large part to behaviors that are seen as socially unacceptable, such as impulsivity, high levels of frustration, and failure to interpret nonverbal cues. Ten-year-old Alice, who has a learning disability, displayed poor social skills that caused her to alienate her peers. She frequently talked too much. Her peers went so far as to call her "the Mouth" because of her nonstop talking and her lack of tact. Sometimes Alice would tell a joke repeatedly, trying to hold her audience. She also unwittingly insulted her listeners. Alice, who had a learning disability, did not notice how the expressions on her listeners' faces changed as she talked, nor was she aware of signs of boredom, disinterest, or irritation. She had few friends, and she was usually not invited to parties.

Learning disabled children are often extremely disorganized and can annoy and inconvenience their peers. They are often late to appointments, get lost, or forget what they need to bring. For instance, George, a twelve-year-old with a learning disability, exhibited several of these behaviors. One weekend he was invited to go camping with a classmate, an event that was the highlight of George's summer. When the day of the trip arrived, George's father drove him to his friend's house, but along the way George could not remember whether he had to turn left or right into his friend's neighborhood. After several wrong turns, they finally chanced upon the right street, arriving a few minutes late. When George hopped out of the car, he saw that his friend and his friend's parents were angry. George had remembered the wrong time—rather than meeting him at 10 A.M., as he thought, he was expected by 9 A.M. George was over an hour late! And to make matters worse, he discovered while transferring his gear to his friend's car that he had forgotten to pack his sleeping bag. Fortunately, his friend had an extra, so they could get on the road. This friend never invited George for a planned activity again.

Emotional Problems

Emotional stress and low self-esteem can manifest themselves through negative behavior, such as depression, juvenile delinquency, and aggression, which, combined with academic and social problems, may indicate to teachers the need to test for learning disabilities. The academic and social challenges that affect children with learning disabilities have a profound effect on their self-esteem. Self-worth cannot develop when a student is constantly criticized or punished for failing academically and is ridiculed by peers. "School offered me a daily lesson on how inadequate I was,"[13] reveals one individual with a learning disability.

Sometimes low self-esteem leads to feelings of depression and causes some students to withdraw from social interaction or engage in negative activities. By the time some learning-disabled students enter high school, they have experienced so much failure that 35 percent of them drop out of school. Many also look to drugs or alcohol for emotional relief from the depression. One

Some students with learning disabilities become frustrated and withdraw from the social interaction of a classroom.

report found that more than half of teens undergoing treatment for substance abuse have learning disabilities. Martin, who has a learning disability, describes how substance abuse provided an outlet for him at first:

> I had a lot of problems in school from the beginning. . . . I had trouble focusing on what I was reading and I could not take notes. . . . No way was I going to college. . . . By the time I graduated from high school I thought I'd never amount to anything. . . . I always felt like other kids were laughing at me. . . . I just thought everybody hated me and that helped feed this terrific anger I felt all the time. When I was a senior in high school I discovered alcohol and drugs and I felt like my troubles were over. . . . The only trouble was, alcohol made me completely crazy. I was always getting into trouble. I couldn't work steady. . . . I drifted from job to job. . . . At night I'd go to bars and get into fights.[14]

Children with learning disabilities are also at higher risk for becoming juvenile delinquents because of substance abuse problems or unresolved anger that is manifested as criminal behavior. One study found that 50 percent of incarcerated youth had undetected learning disabilities. In addition, it is estimated that 31 percent of learning-disabled youth are arrested within a few years out of high school. New York judge Jeffrey H. Gallet, himself a learning-disabled individual, writes, "Almost every week I see a learning disabled child who, undiagnosed or untreated, is venting his or her frustrations in anti-social ways."[15]

Such antisocial behavior can be expressed as aggression, which may be another sign of underlying emotional problems. Teachers may recognize that children who hit, pinch, push, and constantly fight with peers may be acting out of frustration over academic and social difficulties. Bullies and teens who constantly act tough may also be acting out of frustration and feelings of low self-esteem as a result of their problems in school.

Students will sometimes act tough and aggressive to avoid doing tasks they are not able to do. Richard Strauss, a Dallas real estate manager, tried to hide the fact that he could not read or write as a child by yelling, throwing, slamming, and bothering his classmates. His disruptive behavior resulted in several expulsions, and his parents had to find him another school each time. "I was called lazy, willful, manipulative—and I wasn't," he explains. "I didn't know what was wrong with me. I just knew I was trying hard, and it wasn't working. So then I turned to making mischief because I'd rather be called bad than dumb."[16]

Signs of Hiding the Disability

Teachers also need to be aware that some children with learning disabilities will adopt behavior to hide their problems. One learning-disabled adult explains how he hid his disabilities at school as a child: "I learned to act a certain way so I couldn't be teased. I would appear bored, tired, eager to be of help, all-knowing or funny, depending upon what was going on. In other words, I would do anything but let them know I couldn't read the material."[17] Students use a variety of behaviors to draw attention away from the tasks they cannot do. These behaviors should serve as warning signs to teachers of a possible learning disability.

Teachers should investigate the problems underlying students who perform poorly in academics and yet act as if they know everything. These students usually have a gift of gab and a good memory for facts. Nathan was able to hide his inability to read by listening to lectures and discussions in school and by watching television. He memorized as much information as possible that related to what he was supposed to be reading about in his textbooks. He could verbally express this information from memory in class discussions or oral presentations without having to write it down. His constant boasting about how much he knew disguised the fact that he could not read.

Teachers should notice students who keep a low profile at school by sitting at the back of the class, slouching low in their seats, never volunteering to answer questions or read aloud, and not participating in group activities. One such student describes how she tried to avoid having to read aloud in class. "I would hide in my shell," she said, "[and] hold my neck in like a turtle, almost pleading with the teacher not to call upon me."[18] By hiding in her "shell," or attempting to make herself invisible to the teacher and her classmates, this student tried to keep anyone from noticing her poor speaking and reading abilities.

Students who act as if they do not care about learning or school may also be hiding a learning disability. Teachers should note those students who pretend that they have more important things

Informed teachers can identify kids with learning problems by noticing their frequent, even constant, inattentiveness.

to do with their time, or that they already know the material so they do not need to study it. Karen, who could not write well, was one such student. Her handwriting was illegible and her spelling very poor. She hid this difficulty by refusing to do any written assignments in school. She put on an act for her parents and teachers. She was supposed to write one book report every month on a book of her choice. Karen always read a book, but she would not complete a report. She told her teacher she did not need to write a report to prove she had read a book. She also said she did not care that the lack of book reports brought her grades down. In this way, Karen tried to keep her poor writing skills hidden.

One of the most common behaviors students use to cover up learning disabilities is acting like a clown. Teachers should be aware that these students may be acting funny to draw attention away from the tasks they cannot do. Tyler was known as the class clown because of his goofy antics and jokes in class. He had a clever sense of humor and learned to use it whenever he was called on. His language skills were good, but he could not remember facts, such as names, dates, and places. When he was asked a question that he could not answer, he made up something that would have the class roaring in laughter. Tyler's behavior also made him popular with his peers, which boosted his self-esteem.

It is important that teachers recognize behaviors that may indicate a student is hiding a learning disability. How teachers respond to the academic, social, and emotional behavior of their students often determines whether a learning disability is diagnosed.

Deciding to Evaluate a Student

Once a teacher notices that a student is having academic, social, or emotional problems, the teacher will usually try to help the student solve these problems. A teacher who is trained to recognize the symptoms of a learning disability may have the student evaluated. A teacher who does not know what to look for, however, may respond in ways that unintentionally contribute to the student's learning difficulties.

The importance of a teacher knowing what to look for is illustrated in this example about a young student who was eventually diagnosed with a learning disability. Joey entered kindergarten in Mrs. Brown's class. After a few weeks in school, Mrs. Brown noticed that Joey was having some problems with his schoolwork. She held a conference with his parents and described what she had observed by using some of his artwork as an example. She held up an "elephant" Joey had cut and pasted together. She pointed out that he had not cut on the dotted lines, so the elephant's body parts were misshapen and the edges of the paper were jagged. In addition, he had glued the ears and the trunk on the bottom of the elephant's body, and the misplaced pieces were drowning in a pool of glue. His name was scribbled on the back in barely readable form. Mrs. Brown told Joey's parents that she thought his sloppy work was the result of laziness. She thought that Joey did not care about how his work looked, and that he needed to try harder. As the year progressed, both Mrs. Brown and Joey's parents put pressure on him to try harder and stop being lazy. Joey tried, but his work did not improve. Inside he began to think he must be stupid—what other reason could there be for his lack of improvement? The next year Joey was enrolled in Ms. Green's first-grade class. Ms. Green also noticed Joey's troubles with neatness and met with his parents. However, Ms. Green suggested that Joey's problems with cutting, gluing, and organizing might be the result of a learning disability. In fact, she recognized that his behavior was characteristic of a fine-motor disability. The next step was to have Joey evaluated to find out if he did have a learning disability.

The Evaluation

When teachers recognize the signs of a possible learning disability, they refer the child for further evaluation to a team of specialized professionals who can diagnose learning disabilities. Corinne Smith, a learning-disability specialist, explains why a team evaluation is critical for an appropriate diagnosis: "No one test—and no one individual—can possibly be expected to provide all the information and expertise needed to make these judgements. The law therefore requires public school districts to use multidisciplinary teams of professionals in the identification process."[19]

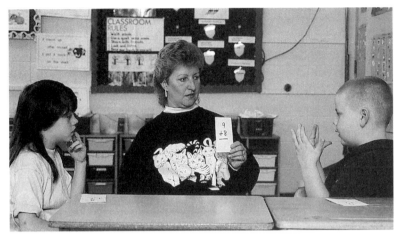

Special education teachers often tackle the more severe cases of learning disability.

In addition to the student's teacher, the team consists of a learning-disability specialist or psychologist, speech-language pathologist, occupational therapist, and the student's physician. The learning-disability specialist evaluates the child's academic proficiency, the psychologist evaluates the child's cognitive (thinking, reasoning, and memory) abilities, and the speech-language pathologist examines the child's spoken and written language skills. The occupational therapist evaluates the child's fine-motor skills, and the teacher is asked to provide input on the child's behavior and academic performance in class. The child's personal physician examines the child's general health and provides a neurological evaluation.

Each of these professionals plays an important role in the evaluation. In addition to the professional assessment tests, the student and his or her parents are interviewed, and the child is observed in the classroom and possibly at home.

The Learning-Disability Specialist or Psychologist

Either a learning-disability specialist or a psychologist will administer a standardized test that measures intellectual capacity. Tests that measure a person's intellectual capacity are called intelligence quotient (IQ) tests. Two of the more commonly used IQ tests are the Wechsler Intelligence Scale for Children, Third Edition (WISC-III), and the Stanford-Binet Intelligence Scale, Fourth Edition (SB:4). The WISC-III is available for testing students between the ages of six and sixteen years old, and it assesses both verbal and nonverbal abilities. During the verbal part of the WISC-III, the child is asked to give factual information, categorize, solve math problems, define words, answer commonsense questions, and is tested for short-term auditory memory. The nonverbal section requires the child to tell what is missing in various pictures, copy marks from a visual code, arrange pictures to tell a story, arrange blocks to match a printed design, and put puzzles together.

The SB:4 is available for testing students ages two to twenty-three years, and it measures abilities in verbal, nonverbal, mathematical reasoning, and short-term memory. During the SB:4 a child is asked to demonstrate skills in vocabulary, reading comprehension, word relationships, patterns, copying, folding and cutting paper, sequencing numbers, solving math problems, and remembering sentences, digits, and objects.

The results of the IQ tests are then compared to a student's academic performance. A significant gap between intelligence and performance might indicate that a child has a learning disability. Although tests such as these are widely used and are accepted as valid by educators, they are not 100 percent accurate all of the time. In fact, some educators are questioning what exactly IQ tests measure.

The Speech-Language Pathologist

The speech-language pathologist (SLP) tests a student's receptive (language that is heard or read and understood) and expressive (language that is spoken or written) language skills. The SLP uses a variety of standardized tests, including the Carrow Elicited Language Inventory (CELI) and the Peabody Picture Vocabulary Test (PPVT).

CELI assesses a student's use of grammatical structures and syntax. It requires the SLP to dictate sentences to the student, who must repeat the sentences back. The word length and syntactic complexity increase as the test is completed. For example,

This girl is taking a Weschler IQ test, which will measure both her verbal and nonverbal skills.

the SLP may give the student a sentence such as "The tiny baby dropped the bottle" (simple) or "The man who is head of the division is going to quit after this week because of the company's financial problems" (more complex).

The PPVT tests the receptive vocabulary of a student. The SLP administers the test by showing the student a large card with four pictures on it. The SLP says a word and the student must point to the picture on the card that is associated with that word. Only one of the four pictures is correct. For instance, one of the cards might have these four pictures shown: a tree under a blue sky and bright sun, a tree under a gray sky and covered with snow, a tree under a blue sky with its branches being blown in one direction, and a tree under a gray sky filled with raindrops and lightning. The SLP then asks the student to point to the picture that shows "rainy." The student must point to one of the four pictures. The SLP notes whether the answer was correct and moves on to the next card. The vocabulary increases in difficulty as they work through the cards.

The Occupational Therapist

The occupational therapist (OT) assesses a student's fine-motor and visual-motor (eye-hand coordination) abilities. The OT uses several tests such as the Bender Visual Motor Gestalt Test and the Bruininks-Oseretsky Test of Motor Proficiency.

The Bender test measures a student's visual-motor skills. It requires the OT to show the student a card with a geometric design on it. The student must copy the design. Once the student has finished drawing the designs from the nine cards, the student is asked to draw all of the designs that he or she can remember.

The Bruininks-Oseretsky test evaluates fine- and gross- (big muscles like arms and legs) motor abilities. It is divided into several subtests, each of which requires the OT to ask the student to perform several gamelike tasks. The gross-motor development tests measure running speed and agility, balance, coordination, and strength in the arms, shoulders, abdomen, and legs, and they also include activities like balancing while standing on one leg. The gross- and fine-motor development tests assess upper limb coordination and include activities such as bouncing and catching a ball. The fine-motor development tests measure upper limb speed and dexterity and visual-motor control, and they require the student to perform tasks like cutting out a circle.

The Physician

The physician examines the child's general health to rule out any medical causes for the difficulties with learning. A physical examination is conducted to evaluate the child's hearing, vision, reflexes, motor coordination, and neurological condition. The neurological condition is assessed using an EEG (electroencephalogram), during which electrodes (wires) are attached to the head to measure brain waves. The child's brain waves are then compared to normal EEGs; if any irregularities are observed then the child is considered to have measurable brain damage. However, most children with learning disabilities show no measurable brain damage in their EEGs. This is important because measurable brain damage can sometimes be controlled with medication, which is a completely different approach and one that does not work with most children who have learning disabilities. Thus, in most cases, the physician's report is used to rule out any observable physical or neurological problems.

Making the Diagnosis

Each team member evaluates the student and the student's work and prepares a report indicating problems or risk factors pointing to a learning disability. Sight or hearing problems and socioeconomic or cultural reasons for the learning problems must also be ruled out. For example, Maria was misidentified as having a learning disability until a visit to her home revealed that her parents spoke only Italian. She had scored poorly on her kindergarten entrance tests not because of a disability but because of a language barrier!

Once the evaluation team members have completed their individual reports, a meeting is held between them, the classroom teacher, and the parents. The purpose of the meeting is to discuss the findings of the evaluation team, collaboratively decide if the student meets the criteria for receiving special-education services in the learning-disability category, and to determine what special-education services and intervention methods are needed. Although qualification criteria can vary between schools and different states, most educators agree that for a student to be considered learning disabled there must be a discrepancy between academic potential as measured by the standardized tests and actual performance as indicated by a student's poor academic achievement. Once the criteria are met and the diagnosis is made, an "intervention" plan is created by the evaluation team and the classroom teacher to help the student cope with the learning disability.

While determining the intervention, it is important to note areas of strength and to determine how the child best learns. It is for this reason that past teaching methods and materials are examined to determine what works and what does not work for the student. Finally, an individualized special-education program is designed to help the student with a learning disability cope with problem areas and improve academic achievement.

Chapter 3

Coping with a
Learning Disability

SINCE THERE IS currently no known medical cures for learning disabilities, children who are diagnosed must learn ways to cope that allow them to accomplish their academic and personal goals. Coping strategies vary from person to person and are based on individual strengths and weaknesses. Coping strategies range from formal teaching techniques to classroom modification, adjusting behavior in social and personal situations, and even include building self-esteem.

Special-Education Programs

When students are identified as having learning disabilities, special-education programs teach them positive coping strategies. All public-school students who are diagnosed as learning disabled will receive some type of special instruction or be allowed classroom modifications. A federal law, which was passed in 1969, requires that these students receive special-education services that meet their individual needs.

Special-education programs usually require the student to receive services in the regular classroom most of the day and in a specialized setting once or twice a week. This means the classroom teacher is primarily responsible for helping the student cope with the learning disability, but a small amount of extra help is provided in another room (such as the learning-disability specialist's room or a resource room) and usually focuses on basic skills remediation. During this time the student either works in a small group of about three or one-on-one with the teacher.

Special tests are administered when parents and school officials believe a child may have a learning disability.

The student gets help with basic skills in this setting, which usually is reading but could also include mathematics.

Students who have language-processing disabilities will spend one-half hour sessions with the speech-language pathologist (SLP) once or twice a week. These sessions may be held in the SLP room or the regular classroom. There are a variety of language activities the SLP may have students participate in depending on their individual needs. For example, Kris, a fourth-grader who has problems with word retrieval, plays word games in which she must think of as many words as possible for a particular picture on a card. If she is shown a picture of an apple, she must think of words to describe an apple, such as *red, juicy, crisp,* and *sweet.* This activity helps Kris improve her ability to retrieve appropriate words.

Students with fine-motor disabilities will spend time outside the regular classroom with the occupational therapist (OT) usually once a week for one-half hour to an hour. During these sessions the OT will have students perform certain tasks, such as cutting, writing, drawing, and picking paper clips up by using their thumbs and forefingers.

The services provided to students by the resource teacher, SLP, or OT are supported in the regular classroom. This means that the classroom teacher must help students continue to practice the skills they are learning from the special-education service providers. For instance, Timmy's teacher outlines all cutting materials in thick black marker so that it is easier for him to cut accurately despite his problems with hand-eye coordination.

Individual Learning Styles

There is no single method that works best when teaching children with learning disabilities. Since disabilities vary by type and degree, the coping strategy must be tailored to suit the needs of the individual student. One way to do this is to design a coping strategy that emphasizes the student's learning style. There are several learning styles, the primary ones being visual (learns by seeing), auditory (learns by hearing), and kinesthetic (learns by doing). Writer Sally L. Smith illustrates this:

> Eleanor cannot remember and dial telephone numbers like the rest of us. Touch-tone telephones have saved her. The knowledge is in her fingertips, which remember the correct configurations. Ben, on the other hand, *sees* telephone numbers as visual patterns on the buttons of the touch-tone phone—as squares, triangles, and rectangles. The keys to teaching Eleanor and Ben lie in understanding their approaches to memory.[20]

Giving students opportunities to learn material by using their primary learning styles greatly enhances their success in accomplishing reading, writing, math, and other academic tasks.

Learning by Association

Learning-disabled students often learn facts or concepts more easily by associating them with something that is already familiar to them. Although many children can remember facts more easily when sung or chanted to a song, rhyme, or poem, utilizing this strategy might be the *only* way some learning-disabled students can memorize information. Sammi, a first-grader with a learning disability, was able to remember the days of the week and the months of the year by singing them to the tune of "Twinkle, Twinkle Little Star." Another student memorized the multiplication tables by chanting them to a favorite rap beat. Patrick had to associate a picture that represented a word in order to read and write the word. For example, he would have to draw a picture of a cat before he could match the spoken form of *cat* with the printed form of *cat*. Somehow the association provides the "missing link" in the brain that causes the learning disability. This missing link can also be overcome by breaking down the learning process into small, sequential steps.

The Orton-Gillingham Method

Whereas most children learn in spite of the way they are taught, those with learning disabilities tend to achieve greater success when teachers use concrete, step-by-step approaches that are repeated many times. Perhaps the most widely used step-by-step

Schoolchildren improve their reading skills by studying phonics from alphabet cards.

method for teaching reading to learning-disabled students is the Orton-Gillingham Method, which emphasizes the learning of sounds and how they fit together to create words. Teachers who use the Orton-Gillingham Method introduce phonics in a series of steps, beginning with the simplest skill and progressing to the most difficult. The Orton-Gillingham Method also requires that reading, spelling, and handwriting be taught at the same time so students are able to apply a skill across all of these language areas.

The first step of the method is to learn to match letter sounds with their symbols. Only one sound at a time is introduced. If students are learning the sound of the letter *b*, they will practice reading, writing, and spelling one-syllable words with the sound of *b* at the beginning of them. For example, they will read the word *bat*, write the word *bat* (by copying it), and spell the word *bat* (they must translate it from the spoken form to the written form). All of the other sounds used in these words will have already been learned—meaning the *a* and *t* sounds in the word *bat* have already been mastered. They will practice using the sound in these three ways in many words, such as *bug, bun*, and *bud* (the *u, g, n*, and *d* sounds will have already been mastered).

After the students master reading, writing, and spelling the *b* sound at the beginning of words, the next step is to practice using it in words that end with *b*, such as *tub, tab*, and *nab.*

Once the students have mastered using all of the sounds of the letters in one-syllable words, they begin a series of steps that teach them to read words put together in simple sentences. For instance, they learn to recognize the word *the* by practicing reading, writing, and spelling sentences like "The dog bit the cat." These steps are continued until students have mastered using all of the words in the curriculum. The end result is that students will gain the decoding skills needed to successfully develop more complex reading and writing abilities.

Betty Freeman, a school principal in Los Angeles, California, credits the Orton-Gillingham Method with helping learning-disabled students in her district learn to read. "I was deeply concerned about students who were not learning to read," she said. "[We] used innumerable reading approaches—but the gains were minimal. I was delighted when the [Orton-Gillingham Method] was introduced. . . . The results were dramatic. Our remedial students learned to read!"[21]

Lindamood-Bell Tutoring

Another successful approach to teaching learning-disabled students to read is Lindamood-Bell tutoring. During the tutoring sessions, students are required to identify how sounds feel while saying them. Sounds are given "names" to help associate them with the action, such as calling *p* a "lip popper" because of the sound that is made when the lips start together and then come apart. The reason why this method works so well is because it gets students past the processing obstacle, which is their inability to break words down into sounds.

Once phonemics (knowing the sounds of letters) are mastered, students develop reading comprehension skills through visualization/verbalization exercises. Students literally learn to see the whole picture in their heads while they are reading by repeating out loud what they have read and visualizing it at the same time. For example, while reading the sentence "The fish swam away," the student would imagine a fish swimming.

The Multisensory Approach

Another way students learn to cope with their learning disabilities is by using a multisensory approach, which is a combination of all learning styles. Teachers who use this approach give students the opportunity to see, hear, touch, smell, and move what they are being taught. They must *be* part of what they are learning in a very literal way. Unlike the VAKT, which was a technique specific to reading, the multisensory approach can be applied to any subject.

The Lab School of Washington, D.C., a special school for learning-disabled children and adults, attempts to teach just about everything in a multisensory way. Students spend only half their day in a classroom and the rest of the day doing art, science labs, and participating in academic clubs. History, for instance, is taught through academic clubs so that children can actually become part of what they are studying. The Middle Ages Club is taught by Lord Don,

Remedial students are encouraged to produce verbal sounds when learning the alphabet.

who "leads" his students, Knight Hal, Lady Rachelle, and others, through a reenacted medieval battle, which is followed by a paint-and-paper recreation of the Bayeaux Tapestry (an actual pictorial account of the Battle of Hastings in 1066 in England). Their final deed is the writing of the Domesday Book, an accounting of property owned in 1086. By immersing themselves in recreating history, these students learn a great deal about medieval life and probably will remember most of what they learn—a far cry from reading a textbook chapter on the same subject! Although more teachers are becoming aware of the value of this approach in teaching all students, despite whether they are learning disabled, it takes a great deal of creativity, time, and energy to turn every reading, math, science, and history lesson into a multisensory experience. Some schools do not have the financial resources to support changes in teaching methods in every classroom.

However, there are ways any teacher can use the multisensory approach with individual students or small groups of students with similar learning disabilities. Susan, a first-grader, has trouble recognizing the letters of the alphabet. Her teacher instructs Susan to say the letters out loud while tracing them in sand, salt, and flour. She also has Susan bend her body in different positions to form the individual letters as she says them. In this way, Susan was finally able to remember the letters. Similarly, Jason, a high-school student who reads very slowly and retains little of the content, creates charts, diagrams, maps, sketches, and other graphic materials to help him retain the information he reads. A kindergartner who cannot remember shapes may benefit from cutting the shapes out, making pictures with the shapes, and playing with three-dimensional shaped objects (such as blocks).

Other multisensory teaching strategies utilize logic labs, invention fairs, cause-and-effect games, and solving mysteries in order to develop hands-on problem-solving skills. One creative teacher who specialized in learning disabilities assigned her students the task of finding a cure for cancer, giving them facts on cards, microscopes, cells to observe, and other science lab materials. Another teacher took her students on a field trip to a nearby polluted pond, let them take pictures of what they observed, and had them write a letter to the utility company responsible for the pollution about ways they could clean up the pond to prevent further damage.

Educational researchers believe the multisensory approach is successful primarily because it allows students to learn using different mediums. In this way students can learn using a medium that gets the information to the brain without being distorted. This means that students who have trouble processing information through a visual medium may be able to learn the information by using an auditory medium instead.

Compensating for a Learning Disability

Sometimes, in spite of special-education services that provide specialized instruction, students with learning disabilities are not able to learn important skills. Some attain only basic literacy (third- to fourth-grade level reading) while others never become good spellers or writers. For some learning-disabled students, mathematics will always remain a mystery. Researchers do not know enough about how the human brain works to understand why some learning-disabled students overcome their difficulties but others do not.

Some sufferers find that by combining audiotaped textbooks with written material their learning ability increases.

For the students who do not find the "missing link" to overcome their disabilities, learning how to compensate for these weaknesses is crucial to success later in life. A learning "crutch"—any behavior that helps students succeed despite their learning disabilities—can help a student compensate for academic difficulties. One student discovered that doodling while listening helped him focus attention on what was being said. A slow reader can use the read-along technique, which means using audiotaped textbooks, workbooks, and literature as a guide to the printed materials.

There are numerous modifications teachers can make in the classroom materials, assignments, and teaching methods. For example, students with learning disabilities can be given more time to answer questions and to complete written work. Those who cannot write well can benefit from copies of notes from lectures or audiotaped recordings. When assigned term papers, students could be allowed to do alternate projects to display their knowledge, like video presentations, maps, dioramas, or dramatizations. Teachers can highlight important information on handouts or assignments, and they should give both oral and written instructions. Visual and kinesthetic aids, such as graphs, charts, blocks, and Legos can be used. Students who have trouble with memorization should be exempted from activities such as memorizing the periodic table of elements or oral math tests.

Access to technology can greatly enhance learning for students with learning disabilities. Computers with word-processing programs allow students to compensate for poor writing and spelling. They also can help with reading, as an increasing number of literature and other printed material is available as read-along text on a computer. "Talking books," books on tape, and educational videos are also available as alternatives to reading. Calculators can help students who have trouble with computations and basic facts but know mathematical concepts. A sixth-grader described how his brothers, who have learning disabilities, compensated for the things they could not do: "One of my brothers has [a] girl in his college class taking notes for him on what is said in class for he spells so bad he can't read his own notes. Then in the subjects that

Computerized spell checkers and calculators assist children with learning disabilities.

he has a lot of reading to do my mother types out notes for him to study. All my brothers use the tape recorder in their classes."[22]

Coping with Social Difficulties

In addition to positive coping strategies for academic success, children with learning disabilities can also be taught how to cope with social problems. Children can be made aware of how they appear to others, and those with weak social skills can improve through role-playing. Students who talk too much, for example, would first role-play being "in the other person's shoes," by listening to someone else talk. In this way, they are made aware of the skills they need to work on. The next step would be for the students to practice taking turns in a conversation, with the teacher standing by to remind them to pause and listen at appropriate times.

To some extent, just achieving greater success academically improves a student's self-confidence, which in turn may improve social experiences. Earl was a young student with a learning disability who complained about every little thing that went wrong in his day. His mornings usually started out on a sour note with him losing his pencil, which made him the subject of jokes among his classmates. Earl did not realize that his constant complaining contributed to the ridicule to which his peers subjected him. In Earl's case, his lack of academic success contributed to his poor self-esteem and social skills. After he was diagnosed and began receiving special-education services, his learning-disability specialist described how his social difficulties improved:

> As I worked with Earl, I noticed that his optimism increased in direct proportion to his improving grades and confidence in himself. . . . Earl's self-esteem and personality improved as his grades did. The time even came when we could laugh about his gripes. . . . His classmates must have noticed the change, too, because one day he appeared for his lesson trailed by a friend.[23]

Self-Regulation Outside of School

Social problems also improve when students with learning disabilities are taught self-regulatory skills. Self-regulation is the ability to control one's space and time, which affects life both inside and outside of school. Children with learning disabilities frequently have trouble with regulating their time and space. It is important for all students to be in control of both their personal belongings and their planned activities throughout the day. Without the ability to control them, belongings will clutter up space and activities will be missed or attended late. Keeping personal space such as bedrooms, desks, and closets organized must often be taught to learning-disabled children. Although it is common for many children to have messy bedrooms, they are able (but not always willing) to clean up their rooms. Children with learning disabilities may be so overwhelmed by the disorganization in their rooms that they do not know where to start. One way to help learning-disabled students regulate their space is to break tasks into smaller steps. One such step-by-step method is the walking-through technique, which involves first showing how a job is done and then actually doing it, over and over, until the job is done. One parent describes how the walking-through technique helped his son on moving day:

> Our child with a learning disability was supposed to join his brothers and sister in organizing each of their respective rooms. However when faced with this task, he became . . . nonfunctional [not able to do anything]. It was not that he rebelled and refused to do the task, it was that he seemed completely puzzled by it. As all the other children put things away, he sat in the middle of the room. . . . He did not . . . know where to start. Finally . . . Granny went in and walked him through the job in the nicest way. She helped him organize his shirts, socks, and pants. She moved him through the organizational maze slowly and patiently until the job was done. . . . All books and clothes had been put away neatly. Both she and my son were very pleased with themselves![24]

A step-by-step method like the walking-through technique can also be used to help learning-disabled students regulate their time. Their days may be filled with activities such as doing homework, studying for a test, packing for a camping trip, attending

Students with learning problems are often disorganized at home, finding even small tasks such as cleaning their room overwhelming.

soccer practice, working an after-school job, or remembering a loved one's birthday. Without help, learning-disabled children may schedule too many activities at one time, forget appointments, or arrive late to engagements. For example, Sharon, the mother of a learning-disabled boy named Josh, felt frustrated with her son's poor sense of time management. He did not get up for school on time, was often late to his after-school job, and left his clothes and books scattered everywhere throughout the house. For years Sharon picked up the slack by making sure Josh's alarm was set every night and by pulling him out of bed in the morning. When he called after school in a panic because he forgot that he had to be at work at 3:00 P.M. instead of 4:00 P.M., she rushed to school, picked him up, and rushed him to work. Every afternoon she collected his things around the house and deposited them neatly in his room. By the time he reached eleventh grade, Sharon realized that her son was not going to grow out of this, and that if he was ever going to be a responsible adult, she had to stop being responsible for him.

Sharon helped Josh learn responsibility by posting a collaborative list on his bedroom door. The list broke down all of the tasks he needed to do when he came home from school each day into steps. First, he was to go from room to room collecting his things and then place them in his bedroom. Next, he had to review his work schedule (posted next to the list) and then check the calendar (also next to the list) to see what other activities he had scheduled that day. As for getting up on time in the morning, Josh put a note in bold letters on his pillow reminding him to set the alarm clock for the next morning. He also disabled the snooze button so he could not keep turning the alarm off, and he placed the clock far enough away that he had to get out of bed to turn it off. By doing this, Josh began to regulate his own time in an effective manner. As students improve control of their behavior, they begin to build confidence in their learning abilities.

Achieving Self-Esteem

Although special education and various coping methods do not "cure" a disability, they can build self-esteem, making it easier for people to deal with the challenges they face on a daily basis. The single most important ingredient for the growth of self-esteem is success. It does not have to come in big doses or even in the form of academic success. Some learning-disabled children find their niche in special talents or gifts. Sarah, who has an auditory language-processing disability, could not remember things people said to her, but she did have an excellent memory for music. Her musical talents gave her confidence in herself even when she felt she was failing in every other area, including academics and her social life.

In junior high school, Sarah became aware of her love for music, and she discovered that she enjoyed both band and chorus. Her music teachers encouraged her to develop her talents. In eighth grade, her self-esteem was boosted when she was chosen to play flute in the second seat in the high-school band. From that point on music turned her life completely around. Sarah went on to join the pep band, the marching band, and the concert orchestra. In addition, she participated in three different choral groups

Children with learning disabilities often channel their energies into music or other non-academic activities to attain self-esteem.

and sang and acted in musical theater performances, winning awards for musical achievement. The highlight of these experiences occurred when she was selected to play the featured solo at the Epcot Center at Disney World while her band was performing there on invitation. All of this success brought one added benefit to Sarah's life, however, as she explains:

> The amazing thing, though, was the way success in music carried over to my other studies. At some point it clicked that I was successful in music *because I worked at it*—and that working hard could make a difference in my other classes. I started to apply myself, and my grades went up. When I graduated, my first-choice college awarded me an academic scholarship.[25]

As Sarah's experience proves, just a little success can go a long way. Building self-esteem can help children with learning disabilities improve their achievement in many areas. Because children do not grow out of learning disabilities, the growing-up years must provide them with confidence in their abilities as well as a basic understanding of what they can and cannot do in order to achieve personal and vocational goals as adults.

Chapter 4

Adults Living and Working with Learning Disabilities

CHILDREN WITH LEARNING disabilities eventually grow up and become adults with learning disabilities. For those individuals who were diagnosed and learned to cope as children, accomplishing their vocational and personal goals is a reasonable expectation. However, they continue to face challenges in education, work, and family, and they must learn to be their own best advocates in getting their needs met.

Unfortunately, not all adults who have learning disabilities were diagnosed as children. Many grew up and struggled through the challenges of adulthood without knowing the reasons behind their unique struggles. As the public has become more aware of learning disabilities, more adults are coming forward and asking for help. They are being diagnosed and taught how to cope with their disabilities at any age.

Warning Signs of Learning Disabilities in Adults

Although many individuals with learning disabilities are diagnosed as children, growing numbers of adults are just discovering their disabilities. Most of these adults grew up before the 1970s, when learning disabilities were first being diagnosed in schoolchildren. Other adults simply slipped through the system unidentified, perhaps because of inadequate evaluations or the educational staff's lack of training to recognize learning disabilities.

Today the public is becoming more aware of learning disabilities and the characteristic behaviors that they entail. As a result, many adults are recognizing these characteristics in themselves or someone close to them, such as a spouse, parent, or friend. Henry was an adult who had slipped through the public-school system in the days before they tested for learning disabilities. Henry had never been able to keep a job, and he had wandered from construction to gardening to factory work. He could not read or write, but because he had traveled all over the United States, he had acquired a lot of knowledge from experience. Self-conscious about his illiteracy, however, Henry kept to himself and appeared slow to his co-workers. Henry's behavior indicated some of the warning signs of an adult with a learning disability. Other signs that an adult may have a learning disability are difficulties with math calculations or concepts, following schedules, being on time, meeting deadlines, following maps, balancing checkbooks, following directions, and telling or understanding jokes.

Some adults have suffered from learning deficiencies all their lives, but are just now understanding the reasons for their struggles.

Reasons for Seeking Help

Usually adults who display the warning signs of learning disabilities have been aware of their academic and social problems since childhood. They have not, however, understood the root of these problems, which usually led them to question their own intelligence or abilities. At some point an event or a revelation may motivate adults to seek professional help for their problems.

In Henry's case, when he eventually saw his four-year-old son beginning to read, he wanted to be able to share stories with him. Henry also thought that if a four-year-old could learn to read, so could he. This propelled him to seek a professional evaluation, which in turn helped him find a school for adults with learning disabilities.

Many adults with learning disabilities seek out help for problems they are having at work. Such problems may include difficulty with interpersonal relationships or poor writing, speaking, or organization skills. Often they do not realize the problems might be the result of a learning disability. After they seek out professional help (usually from a psychologist or educator), they are frequently referred for testing to determine whether they have learning disabilities. For example, Jim was a successful financial executive, but for years he struggled to hide his inability to spell even simple words. The stress finally became too much for him, and he desperately called a friend of his who was a teacher and confessed the truth to her. Fortunately for Jim, his friend explained that his problems sounded similar to a learning disability. She gave him the name of a psychologist who tested adults for learning disabilities. Jim made an appointment to be tested the next week. Public awareness about learning disabilities has prompted many individuals like Henry and Jim to seek a diagnosis for their problems.

Diagnosing Learning Disabilities in Adults

Once adults decide to seek professional help for their suspected disabilities, the next step is to choose who will carry out the evaluation. A variety of sources provide adult evaluations, including neurologists, psychologists, and educational therapists. In California, many community colleges also provide testing to diagnose learning disabilities.

Adults undergo evaluations that are similar to those of children, although only one professional may be responsible for the entire process. The chosen professional administers standardized tests such as the Wechsler Adult Intelligence Scale, Third Edition (WAIS-III), and the Woodcock Reading Mastery Tests, Revised (WRMT-R NU), two of the most commonly used tests in adult assessments. The WAIS-III is similar to the children's version, testing both verbal and nonverbal skills. The WRMT-R NU tests skills in reading comprehension, word decoding, and phonemic awareness (knowing the sounds of letters). The results of these tests may indicate what types of learning disabilities are present.

In addition, the professional will request information about the adult's work, education, and family history. Information about keeping or obtaining jobs, interpersonal relationships with colleagues, and fulfilling job requirements can reveal behaviors associated with a learning disability. Equally important is information about an adult's difficulties in school, social problems with peers or a lack of friendships, and past success in accom-

The IQ tests given to adults are very similar to those administered to children.

plishing educational goals. Reporting that other family members, such as parents, siblings, or children, have similar difficulties may also provide evidence of a learning disability in an adult.

Once the testing is complete and the work, education, and family information has been reviewed, professionals provide reports to the adults detailing the evaluation findings, including a diagnosis of the specific learning disability. The reports become the basis for helping adults learn to cope with their disabilities so they are able to accomplish their personal and vocational goals.

Teaching Adults to Cope with Learning Disabilities

Adults can learn to cope through a number of resources. They can get help from learning-disability specialists or educational therapists who provide private tutoring and counseling. They can also enroll in schools or courses specifically designed for the learning-disabled adult. After Henry was diagnosed, the school that evaluated him was able to teach him to read at an eighth-grade level within two years. Eventually Henry took a study course and enrolled in college as a business student. Many community colleges in California offer effective programs that teach adults with learning disabilities how to read, write, and speak fluently. They also teach them how to compensate for their disabilities if they cannot overcome them.

Lindamood-Bell tutoring, which is also used with children, has proven especially successful with teaching adults with learning disabilities to read. The best community-college programs offer Lindamood-Bell tutoring, which targets reading skills, comprehension, and spelling while teaching adult students strategies for compensating for skills that continue to be difficult. The Lindamood-Bell method is usually provided once a week for four hours for as many weeks as the student needs it.

Adults with learning disabilities may be able to get help through private tutoring, therapy, or adult education classes. Santa Barbara City College in California provides one of the best adult learning-disability programs in the state. Adults may take courses in reading, writing, speaking, and mathematics. Moreover, there are opportunities to learn compensatory skills through the self-advocacy class

Senior citizens volunteer to assist adults diagnosed with learning disabilities.

and courses that teach adults how to use assistive technology, such as computers and audiotapes, to help them succeed at work or in school. For many learning-disabled adults, learning the literacy or compensatory skills they never had before opens the door to a new future. Some of these adults decide to continue their education at college, where they face many of the same challenges that college students who were diagnosed as children do.

Succeeding in College

Most prospective college students must take a standardized college admissions test, such as the Scholastic Assessment Test (SAT) or the American College Testing Assessment Test (ACT). Almost all colleges require scores from one of these tests for admission. The SAT tests students in math and verbal skills while the ACT tests in the areas of reading, math, English, and science. Students who have documented learning disabilities may take these tests with individually determined accommodations, which may include individual administration of the test, using a large print or audiotaped version of the test, special answer sheets, or extended testing time. Myra, who was diagnosed with a learning disability in middle school, was allowed to take the

SAT test in a separate place and was given extra time to read and answer the questions. Paul, who also was diagnosed with a learning disability in middle school, took the SAT in the regular setting but was allowed to circle his answers in the test booklet instead of filling out bubbles on a scan sheet, which would have left him hopelessly confused.

Some colleges have counselors, support groups, or learning-disability services departments on campus that provide resources, counseling, and help with accommodations to learning-disabled students. Not all colleges have such programs in place, however, and even among those that do, some are more helpful than others. For this reason, it is important for prospective college students who have learning disabilities to research the colleges of choice to be certain they offer services and resources to meet their individual needs.

Once in college, learning-disabled students must be assertive about getting their needs met. They must speak up about what these needs are so that professors and fellow students understand their situations. If they do not, the following story illustrates what could happen:

A student handed in her best paper to date to a university teacher who glanced at the paper, threw it back at her, and said, in front of other students, "This is not college material! Why are you here?" The college student had the thinking skills of a gifted adult but, because of her learning disabilities, the writing skills of a fifth grader.[26]

The student in the example should have had access to assistive technology or a tutor to help with writing difficulties. By law, students with documented learning disabilities are entitled to accommodations that support their academic success. Although these should be tailored to individual needs, colleges typically provide several types of accommodations to students with learning disabilities. These may include extending testing times, access to note-takers, modified assignments, alternative testing formats, course waivers or substitutions, and access to assistive technology such as laptop computers or tape recorders.

Learning-disabled college students can attend certain universities which provide counseling and support groups.

Some of these accommodations require students to discuss their learning disabilities with each professor in each college course. For example, a student who reads slowly and has trouble with written expression may ask a professor for extra time to complete a midterm or final exam. This same student might fulfill a research project by giving an oral presentation to the class rather than submitting a written report. For instance, during her senior year in college, Jill was required to take a class in statistics for graduation. She had always had poor math skills, and she found memorizing formulas for calculations almost impossible. Jill discussed the situation with her professor, who agreed to allow Jill to use a "cheat sheet" during tests. The cheat sheet listed all of the formulas for computing statistics, but it still required Jill to apply those formulas and solve the answers herself.

Sometimes colleges will allow students with learning disabilities to waive or substitute a course that is not essential to their major field of study. However, many colleges prefer to substitute one course with another rather than waive a course completely in order to preserve high academic standards. For instance, a student who has a language-processing disability may ask the college to waive the requirement for taking a course in foreign language. The college, however, decides that the student may substitute the foreign language course with a course that covers another culture, which will provide the student with a similar learning experience.

College students with learning disabilities may take advantage of assistive technology that can help them succeed in their classes. Cathy, a college junior with a poor auditory memory, uses a tape recorder to record every two-and-a-half-hour class she takes and then recopies the lectures word for word to help her remember the content. Even though it takes her five or six hours to copy each tape, afterward she rereads the material, highlighting important points. She then goes back and studies it again, until she remembers the material well. Students who are poor writers can compose reports or essays on computers with advanced spelling and grammar features. Those with reading problems can use books on tape to read text material or literature.

Many colleges offer services to students with learning disabilities through a professional staff on campus. These services may include personal and academic counseling, help with determining and obtaining accommodations, and tutoring in reading, writing, math, or specifically requested courses. Academic counselors may advise students to take smaller class loads and allow more time to finish degree programs. They may also provide note takers, who attend classes with students and take notes for them. Note takers will type up the notes and organize them in a clear and distinct manner suitable to the individual's learning style.

Often students with learning disabilities enlist the help of friends and family members while in college. Throughout her college years, one dyslexic young woman, who was a gifted law student, had her mother read every college text to her and help her with writing as well. Jeffrey H. Gallet, a New York judge with a learning disability, recalls the most important factor that got him through law school:

> I wanted to go to law school against the best advice of my
> school counselors. . . . Brooklyn Law School took a chance on

me. I responded with the best academic performance of my career. I graduated in the middle of my class. By law school I had begun to learn how to compensate for my problems [mainly because I] had the good fortune of meeting . . . another student [his roommate] who was willing to spend many hours discussing legal concepts with me.[27]

Gallet also credited his roommate with keeping his confidence up and not allowing him to give up. It is important for college students with learning disabilities to have someone who is available to help them with areas of academic weaknesses as well as to support them emotionally.

Succeeding at Work

Like school, it is important for working adults with learning disabilities to find jobs that utilize their strengths and not their weaknesses. Florence Haseltine, a learning-disabilities educational professional, recommends that adults with learning disabilities should "find out what you cannot do, and discard it. Find another way."[28] For example, Doreen's experience proves the wisdom of Haseltine's advice. Doreen was an outgoing young woman who obtained a job as a school library assistant. However, her training session did not go well because she frequently reversed numbers and was overwhelmed by trying to put books back in the proper place. Fortunately, Doreen told her supervisor that she had a learning disability. She was then placed in a position that used her verbal talents, and eventually Doreen created a popular after-school storytelling program. For adults with learning disabilities, finding a career that caters to their strengths can mean the difference between keeping or losing a job.

An important strategy for adults with learning disabilities is to speak up about what accommodations they need to help them complete a job successfully. This often means being willing to ask colleagues and supervisors to accommodate their needs, as Frank Dunkle, who became director of the U.S. Fish and Wildlife Service in 1986, did. Dunkle could not cope with long briefing papers and asked for one-page summaries instead. "Nobody re-

Frank Dunkle serves as director of the U.S. Fish and Wildlife Service despite suffering from a learning disability.

ally believed me when I told the staff they had a . . . different kind of director," Dunkle said. "I could not cope with the acronyms [words formed from beginning letters of a compound term] . . . so I asked them to please say the words for the letters. I needed to develop my own method of organization to do the best job possible!"[29]

Another compensatory strategy that has benefited some working adults with learning disabilities is exchanging work with colleagues. They find co-workers who need help with tasks they can perform, and then they ask their co-workers to do things they cannot do. Prominent real estate broker Richard Strauss surrounds himself with staff members who do the things he cannot. He dictates what he wants written to his secretary, and other staff members read contracts and financial statements to him. Mark Torrance also uses the work-exchange strategy. A former chief executive officer of Muzak Corporation, he describes how his staff helps him overcome his learning disability: "My . . . staff, they all work around me, and they don't let me do certain things that they know I'm poor at. . . . My secretary won't let me dial the phone because if it's long distance, I get the wrong number all the time."[30]

Adults who have learning disabilities cannot always depend on others to do their difficult tasks at work, however. Sometimes the task is an essential element of their job, such as writing a report or balancing accounts. In such cases, they must find ways of getting a job done that works for them. This could mean taking extra time to do a task or taking on only one or two tasks at a time. Learning-disabled adults may spend a lot more time working than everyone else just to get the job done. They must develop strategies for helping them remember important facts, such as price sheets or procedures. Extra practice in filling out forms during nonwork hours can greatly reduce the time it takes to fill them out on the job later.

As more adults come forward to be tested and taught how to cope with their disabilities, even faces familiar to the American public have begun to speak publicly about their learning disabilities. These public figures have become advocates for all people, young or old, living with learning disabilities.

Cher: From Class Clown to Academy Award–Winner

Academy Award–winning actress and singer Cher professed to being a class clown in school to draw attention away from the fact that she could not read, write, or do math. When Cher attended school in the 1950s and 1960s, most educators were not trained to recognize learning disabilities and did not test for them. Her teachers admonished her to try harder, to apply herself better. Cher tried to draw attention away from her academic problems by acting outrageous in class. Her peers thought she was hilarious, and she became well liked for her antics, which encouraged her behavior.

In private, she sang and danced as a way of coping with emotional strains at school. "From the time I could talk, I began to sing," Cher recalls. "Singing just came from the inside—something I'd do without thinking whenever I felt good or was really blue. Dancing? Well, it released my tensions."[31] However, as her reading and math difficulties continued through high school, Cher became convinced that she was stupid and dropped out at age sixteen.

Despite a learning problem which prevents her from reading scripts or lyrics, Cher has memorized her way through an award-winning acting and singing career.

Cher knew that she had a flair for the creative and dramatic, though, and she decided to try to make a career out it. She learned to compensate for not being able to read songs or scripts by listening to others read them and then memorizing the words. She could also create songs in her head and remember them without writing them down. Although she was able to cope with her disabilities, for many years Cher suffered from feelings of self-doubt and low self-esteem. She hid her inability to read and write from everyone, including her family.

As her daughter, Chastity, struggled through school, Cher gradually recognized that they shared many of the same academic problems. She had Chastity tested for learning disabilities by her school, and after she was diagnosed with dyslexia, Cher finally decided to open up about her own problems. At the age of thirty, Cher was also diagnosed with dyslexia.

In the almost two decades since her diagnosis, Cher has spoken publicly about her disabilities. She emphasizes the importance of recognizing the strengths of people with learning disabilities and that they can capitalize on these strengths to be successful in spite of their disabilities.

A Success Story

Along with Cher, many others, celebrities and noncelebrities alike, have joined in spreading the message that people with learning disabilities *can* accomplish their dreams. Joan Esposito is another learning-disabled advocate who is helping to spread this message by sharing her story in speeches and lectures all over the United States. In her speeches she describes the pain of not knowing what was "wrong" with her, of trying to hide her problems from the world, and how she finally overcame them.

Because of her learning disabilities, Esposito has trouble retrieving information quickly from memory, and she has difficulty organizing and expressing her thoughts in sequence. Until she was forty-four years old, she could read only at a fourth-grade level, could not spell, and her punctuation and grammar skills were at the first-grade level. Esposito describes her early life struggling with an undiagnosed learning disability:

> As a young child . . . the time that I spent attending classes and attempting to learn was literally hell. Every morning I woke up sick to my stomach at the thought of school. . . . Because I did not learn like many of my classmates, I did not socialize with them either. . . . I was constantly teased. . . . I lied and cheated my way through school.[32]

Joan goes on to describe how far she was willing to go to hide her disabilities. The first week that she was married to her first husband, a Beverly Hills literary agent, she was asked to prepare a dinner for some of his clients at their home. Although Joan protested that she did not know how to cook, her husband directed her to several cookbooks in the kitchen. "What I didn't confess was that I couldn't read them," Joan explains. "I managed to talk my new husband into cooking the meal."[33] She took a French cooking class to keep her reading problem a secret, however. She watched the chef prepare a meal and then went

Being learning-disabled, Joan Esposito endured a lifetime of low self-esteem before founding the Dyslexia Awareness and Resource Center.

home and immediately cooked the same meal to remember it. In this way, she was able to learn a recipe without reading it.

Joan's learning disability also affected her social life. Once, while at a party, where she was about to play a word game, she heard that she would have to write down five nouns. She excused herself and went to the bathroom instead. "I walked back and forth, looking in the mirror, and told myself how stupid I was," Joan later recalled. "I had been told over and over what a noun was; why could I not remember? I felt sick to my stomach. I stayed in the bathroom as long as I could and hoped that they had finished their game without me."[34] However, when Joan came out of the bathroom, she found the party had waited for her.

Esposito became very clever about hiding her disabilities, but the effort exacted a physical toll. She was admitted to the hospital several times for violent stomach pains and headaches. She gradually became a recluse, refusing to answer the telephone or leave the house. When friends came to visit, she would stay in her bedroom and pretend that she was ill.

Later, during divorce proceedings, Esposito's husband used her lack of education against her in court to try to gain custody of their son. It was during these court sessions that she was forced to face her problems for the first time. She describes the pain of this experience in her speeches: "Some of the most humiliating experiences of my life came when I sat in . . . courtrooms full of strangers while my illiteracy and lack of a formal education was brought up over and over again."[35] After the divorce, she did not have the necessary skills to get a job with a livable wage, and she was forced to clean hotel rooms to support herself and her son.

Seven years later, Esposito remarried. Only months later, she and her new husband, Les, discovered that Esposito's son had dyslexia and attention deficit disorder (ADD). Recognizing the same problems in herself, Esposito sought out testing and discovered that she had, like her son, dyslexia and ADD. However, getting a diagnosis was just the first step in rebuilding her life. Esposito also had to learn how to cope with her disabilities. "I was forty-four years old, functionally illiterate and full [of] low self esteem," she remembers. "At [Santa Barbara City College] I discovered that I *could* learn to read and write and met other people who function like I do."[36]

Joan Esposito went on to found the Dyslexia Awareness and Resource Center, a nonprofit organization that provides free educational consulting services to parents, children, and adults regarding dyslexia and ADD. The center also provides consulting services during court and probation hearings for juvenile delinquents with learning disabilities. In addition, the center conducts awareness seminars for employers and trains counselors, educators, health professionals, and law enforcement officers in recognizing and dealing with individuals who have learning disabilities and ADD. It is Esposito's hope that by raising awareness of these disabilities some of the controversy surrounding them will be resolved.

Chapter 5

Current Controversies

L EARNING DISABILITIES ARE the subject of a variety of disagreements among educators, researchers, and the public. The lack of a single, standard profile for a learning disability causes disagreement about the validity of IQ tests, varying criteria for diagnosis in schools, a debate about what influence the social environment has on a learning disability, and conflict about whether attention deficit disorders should be classified as a type of learning disability.

Are IQ Tests Accurate?

Since most IQ tests are heavily language-based, students who have language-processing disabilities are going to have difficulties with them. Michael E. Spagna, an educational researcher, explains this problem:

> If you think about intelligence tests, they are language-loaded. So, a child who might have language deficits as a result of his/her reading problem . . . will do poorly on an intelligence test. Is that child going to be diagnosed dyslexic? NO; because [the IQ test makes it look like their poor academic skills are the result of below-average intelligence]. They might have had a big gap between aptitude [intelligence] and achievement if they were tested when they were young, but as they got older, the discrepancy [difference] no longer exists. So, in this instance, I would say that . . . you would have to really ask, "What is the intelligence test testing?"[37]

Thus, the test does not always accurately measure a student's intellectual abilities but only their language-processing abilities. Without that gap between intellectual ability and performance, a student cannot qualify for special-education services. It is unfortunate that they are denied services when in fact they do have a discrepancy between potential and performance. In such cases, the learning disability is not diagnosed and the student does not receive appropriate help.

Another problem with IQ tests is that they only measure certain types of intelligence while ignoring others. Linguistic and logical mathematical intelligences are the only types currently measured on such tests. Some psychologists and educational researchers are requesting that traditional tests be supplemented with others that measure intelligence in music, spatial abilities (used in art, sculpture, and architecture), bodily-kinesthetic abilities (used in dance and athletics), leadership, and empathy (used in psychology, teaching, healing, and social work). Recognizing a capacity in each type of intelligence does more than simply reveal hidden individual talents—it can also reveal the secret to how an individual best learns, an essential part of the diagnostic process. However, while these supplemental tests have gained significant support from many professionals, it takes time to change a system that has been using one type of IQ test for decades.

Questions have arisen as to the validity of IQ tests administered to sufferers of learning disabilities.

Is Diagnosis Accurate?

In addition to questions about the validity of some IQ tests, the presence of other problems, such as hearing or vision loss or language barriers, can make an accurate diagnosis of a learning disability difficult. There is also a tendency in some schools to label any child who has academic, social, or emotional problems not directly attributable to a condition (such as Down's syndrome or deafness) as "learning disabled" (LD).

Children who have emotional problems, for example, are supposed to receive special-education services under the label "serious emotional disturbance" (SED). However, in some cases it is not clear whether the emotional problems are causing the learning difficulties or if a learning disability is the root of the emotional problems. Although no reliable statistics exist for how many children are misdiagnosed in either category, it is common for educators within a single school to debate this question over a single student. Since there is no clear-cut method to distinguish between the two, it is up to the evaluation team to judge whether a student needs SED or LD services.

Problems with labeling may also occur when students have a sensory impairment, such as deafness, hearing loss, or blindness. Ana's case illustrates an example of this situation. By the time Ana was in the second grade, her parents and teachers were concerned about her lack of progress in nearly every school subject. She had trouble with reading, writing, math, science, and social studies. Her teachers knew that she had had a moderate hearing loss since birth, but they suspected that some of her academic difficulties were not related to her hearing problems. Tests showed that Ana had an above-average IQ, but her reading comprehension and written-expression skills were poor. The evaluation team struggled to decide if Ana's academic problems were the result of a language-processing disability or if her language-expression skills were simply delayed because she could not hear well. Both of these factors could cause Ana to have difficulty in reading and writing, which would then affect other academic areas that require reading. The evaluation team finally decided that her academic problems were the result of a language-processing disability that placed her in the LD category. This was the only way that Ana would be eligible to receive services to help her cope with her reading and writing difficulties.

Currently educators have no answers to the problems surrounding the diagnosis of learning disabilities. By nature, learning disabilities overlap with the characteristics of many other types of disabilities, making a definite diagnosis very difficult. In response to this dilemma, educators tend to place students who have no definite cause for their learning problems in the LD category. Educational researcher Michael E. Spagna explains the reasons for such decisions:

> Teachers and administrators are faced with a very hard decision: "I have these students who do not meet the criteria exactly but they're not making it in my class/school. What am I going to do?" Simply put, many youngsters are identified as LD [learning disabled] because this is an avenue to provide educational assistance; without the label, teachers and administrators are faced with the very real alternative—early drop out.[38]

The questions surrounding the appropriate diagnosis of learning-disabled students are further complicated by professionals who believe that learning disabilities are, at least in part, the result of social influences.

Are Learning Disabilities the Result of the Social Environment?

Despite the growing medical research that supports a neurological cause for learning disabilities, some psychologists, educators, and sociologists believe that a person's social environment is partly responsible for the existence of a learning disability. These professionals believe that learning disabilities are partly caused by the demands of school or employment, not biological reasons.

These professionals believe that weaknesses become more pronounced in response to the perceived negative reactions of others. For example, Dennis, a thirty-five-year-old with a learning disability, finds speaking fluently during meetings and presentations challenging. Some professionals would ex-

Learning-disabled professionals often have trouble addressing groups.

plain that his difficulties result from past negative experiences with speaking in front of groups. In other words, when Dennis started his job he may have been nervous about speaking in front of his colleagues because he was afraid of saying the wrong thing or that he would forget what he was supposed to be discussing. During the first meeting he attended, Dennis was asked to speak about the status of the report he was writing. He was nervous and had trouble remembering the new terms he was using in the report. He thought he sounded disorganized and noticed a few colleagues squirm uncomfortably behind the conference table. The next time Dennis attended a meeting he visualized the same scenario happening again, and he worked himself into a state of anxiety by the time his turn to speak arrived. This time around, he was completely at a loss for words. Excusing himself, he mumbled something about having a scratchy throat and escaped to the rest room. After this it seemed to Dennis that he "botched" every speaking opportunity he had at work. His speaking problems resulted in his being passed up for promotions. This in turn reinforced Dennis's view of himself as unable to speak fluently.

Some would attribute Dennis's speaking difficulties to his increasingly anxious reactions to each experience based on how he thought others saw him. Negative experience built on negative experience, trapping Dennis in a cycle of behavior. However, educators and medical researchers who disagree with this theory point out that although social behavior may, in fact, influence how individuals cope with their learning disabilities, it does not explain why or how the cycle starts in the first place. Dennis's self-doubt and anxiety may have contributed to his speaking difficulties, but why did this cycle of behavior start? Learning-disability specialists point out that people who have trouble with word retrieval and organizing words into sentences are going to have problems expressing themselves verbally despite whether they are nervous.

Although most educators and researchers believe that learning disabilities have biological causes, they do not agree to what extent the social environment plays in the behavior of individuals with learning disabilities.

Attention Disorders: Are They a Learning Disability?

Another disagreement occurs between many parents and others in the lay community and most professionals, including educators and researchers, who do not consider attention disorders to be a specific type of learning disability. No one disputes the fact that attention disorders frequently occur along with learning disabilities, but it is a matter of debate whether the attention disorder is to blame for the learning problems or if it is just another condition that complicates learning disabilities much in the same way that a hearing loss or a language barrier would. Attention disorders such as attention deficit disorder (ADD) and attention deficit hyperactivity disorder (ADHD) are the most common among schoolchildren.

ADD is a neurological disability that causes an individual to have a short attention span, difficulty focusing on a task, and impulsive, often inappropriate, behavior. When hyperactivity is also present, the disorder is identified as ADHD. Children with

ADD often fidget with their hands and feet and have trouble sitting still or playing quietly. They frequently do not follow through on instructions, and they shift from one incomplete task to another. Impulsivity causes them to interrupt conversations and ongoing activities such as games. Betty B. Osman, a learning-disability specialist, describes the behavior of one of her students, who had an attention disorder:

> [Some learning-disabled] youngsters . . . are impulsive and easily distracted. This is what . . . makes it hard for them to stick with any game for more than five minutes. . . . Jack was like that. He would entice a friend to play checkers or dominoes but could not stay with it for more than two turns. Jack would then decide that he didn't want to play that "silly game" after all and would suggest something else. Eventually the friend's head would be swimming with the constant change of activities, and that would be the end of the relationship. . . . I remember that even in my office I had to change activities every ten minutes or so to keep his interest. Otherwise he'd begin to look around, ready to dart away at the slightest noise or interruption.[39]

Children with ADD are often observed squirming in their seats, abandoning projects quickly, and paying little attention to work placed before them.

Jack's problems focusing and completing a task caused him to miss important information about assignments, have poor reading comprehension, and routinely turn in incomplete work. Many parents would argue that Jack's academic problems were the result of his ADD and thus constituted a learning disability. Although it is true that Jack's ADD did cause him problems in his academic performance, it did not impair his ability to learn, only his performance.

Professionals who do not consider ADD or ADHD to be learning disabilities point out that, although they can impact students' learning, they are not characterized by neurological problems that cause information-processing disabilities. Rather, attention disorders are the result of differences in the body's metabolism, or the process by which the body uses its energy resources from foods and beverages. The brains of persons with ADD and ADHD use glucose (a naturally occurring sugar found in many foods), which is the brain's primary energy source, in smaller amounts than the brains of persons without attention disorders. Moreover, the reduced glucose use occurs primarily in the part of the brain that controls attention, handwriting, motor control, and the ability to inhibit responses.

Unlike learning disabilities, the metabolic problems that cause ADD and ADHD can be controlled by drugs called psychostimulants. This type of drug stimulates the production of brain chemicals that are needed to carry messages to the affected brain areas, acting as a substitute for the glucose. Nearly 80 percent of children with attention disorders respond positively to these drugs, which decrease motor activity, improve attention spans, and decrease impulsivity and distractibility, all of which improve motivation, accuracy, and achievement in these students. The most common psychostimulants used to treat ADD and ADHD are Ritalin, Dexedrine, and Cylert. Although some educators, physicians, and parents express concern about the long-term side effects from these drugs, current research shows no evidence of harmful effects, such as growth suppression, from their use.

Despite the research that indicates attention disorders are not a specific type of learning disability, the fact that they prevent students from achieving their full academic potential and their

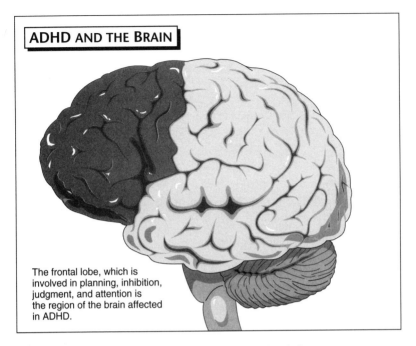

ADHD AND THE BRAIN

The frontal lobe, which is involved in planning, inhibition, judgment, and attention is the region of the brain affected in ADHD.

frequent occurrence along with learning disabilities perpetuates the belief that ADD and ADHD are actually learning disabilities. It is important to note that some children who have ADD without a learning disability may be labeled as such simply because there is no appropriate category under which to place them so they can receive special-education services.

As research continues, the hope remains that scientists will discover more about how the brain works and, specifically, how the brains of persons with learning disabilities work. Perhaps some day science will be able to devise a medical way to provide the "missing link" in the neural pathways so that learning disabilities become a thing of the past. Until then, however, educators must continue to recognize the signs of learning disabilities and help these individuals learn to cope with them in positive ways. This gives them the power to accomplish their goals in life, as this student at the Lab School of Washington, D.C., emphasizes: "I'm going to show the world I can amount to something."[40]

Notes

Introduction

1. Learning Disabilities Association of America, "Through a Child's Eyes," *When Learning Is a Problem.* www.ldanatl.org/pamphlets/learning.shtml.

Chapter 1: History and Types of Learning Disabilities

2. *Saskatchewan Education,* "Challenges, Choices, and Changes," January 1998. www.sasked.gov.sk.ca/k/pecs/se/docs/ccc/9801.html.

3. Corinne Smith and Lisa Strick, *Learning Disabilities A to Z: A Parent's Complete Guide to Learning Disabilities from Preschool to Adulthood.* New York: Simon & Schuster, 1997, pp. 5–6.

4. Quoted in Smith and Strick, *Learning Disabilities A to Z,* pp. 24–25.

5. Quoted in National Institute of Mental Health, press release, "Atypical Brain Activity Detected in People with Dyslexia," July 3, 1996.

6. Quoted in Smith and Strick, *Learning Disabilities A to Z,* p. 78.

7. Quoted in Smith and Strick, *Learning Disabilities A to Z,* p. 80.

8. Quoted in Smith and Strick, *Learning Disabilities A to Z,* pp. 40–41.

9. Quoted in Smith and Strick, *Learning Disabilities A to Z,* p. 58.

10. Quoted in Bryant J. Cratty and Richard L. Goldman, *Learning Disabilities: Contemporary Viewpoints.* Amsterdam, NY: Harwood Academic, 1996, p. 95.

Chapter 2: Diagnosis of Learning Disabilities in Children

11. Quoted in Smith and Strick, *Learning Disabilities A to Z,* p. 9.

12. Quoted in Sally L. Smith, *Succeeding Against the Odds: How the*

Learning Disabled Can Realize Their Promise. New York: Tarcher/Putnam, 1991. p. 41.

13. Quoted in Smith, *Succeeding Against the Odds,* p. 40.

14. Quoted in Smith and Strick, *Learning Disabilities A to Z,* pp. 250–51.

15. Jeffrey H. Gallet, "A Judge's Story," *Gram,* September 1995, pp. 6–9.

16. Quoted in Smith, *Succeeding Against the Odds,* p. 43.

17. Quoted in Editors of Landmark Outreach Program, *Learning Disabilities: Information and Resources.* Prides Crossing, MA: Landmark Outreach Program, 1996, p. 79.

18. Quoted in Editors of Landmark Outreach Program, *Learning Disabilities,* p. 80.

19. Smith and Strick, *Learning Disabilities A to Z,* p. 88.

Chapter 3: Coping with a Learning Disability

20. Smith, *Succeeding Against the Odds,* p. 111.

21. Quoted in *Gram,* "Five Successful Programs for Teaching Reading," September 1995, p. 17.

22. Quoted in Learning Disabilities Association of America, "Through a Child's Eyes."

23. Betty B. Osman, *No One to Play With: The Social Side of Learning Disabilities.* New York: Random House, 1982, pp. 14–15.

24. Quoted in Cratty and Goldman, *Learning Disabilities,* p. 51.

25. Quoted in Smith and Strick, *Learning Disabilities A to Z,* p. 224.

Chapter 4: Adults Living and Working with Learning Disabilities

26. Smith, *Succeeding Against the Odds,* p. 205.

27. Gallet, "A Judge's Story," pp. 6–9.

28. Smith, *Succeeding Against the Odds,* p. 105.

29. Quoted in Smith, *Succeeding Against the Odds,* p. 104.

30. Quoted in Smith, *Succeeding Against the Odds,* pp. 104–105.

31. Quoted in *Time,* "Cher: Cover Story," March 17, 1975, p. 56.

32. Quoted in Cratty and Goldman, *Learning Disabilities,* pp. 204–205.

33. Quoted in Cratty and Goldman, *Learning Disabilities,* p. 206.

34. Quoted in Cratty and Goldman, *Learning Disabilities,* p. 207.

35. Quoted in Cratty and Goldman, *Learning Disabilities,* p. 209.

36. Quoted in Cratty and Goldman, *Learning Disabilities*, p. 210.

Chapter 5: Current Controversies
37. Quoted in Cratty and Goldman, *Learning Disabilities*, p. 120.
38. Quoted in Cratty and Goldman, *Learning Disabilities*, p. 96.
39. Osman, *No One to Play With*, p. 8.
40. Quoted in Smith, *Succeeding Against the Odds*, p. 71.

Organizations to Contact

American Speech-Language-Hearing Association
10801 Rockville Pike
Rockville, MD 20852
(301) 897-5700
Internet: www.asha.org

This organization is a professional, scientific, and credentialing group for audiologists, speech-language pathologists, and language and learning scientists. It provides resources for information on language disorders.

Children and Adults with ADD (CH.A.D.D.)
8181 Professional Pl., Suite 201
Landover, MD 20785
(800) 233-4050
Internet: www.chadd.org

CH.A.D.D. is committed to providing resources and advocacy on attention deficit disorders and how they relate to learning disabilities.

Dyslexia Awareness and Resource Center (DARC)
928 Carpinteria St., Suite 2
Santa Barbara, CA 93103
(805) 963-7339
Internet: www.dyslexia-center.com

The mission of the DARC is to raise awareness of parents, students, adults with dyslexia and/or attention deficit disorder, educators, law enforcement agencies, employers, and health professionals of dyslexia and the characteristics that often accompany dyslexia and attention deficit disorder. It provides literature, video and audiotapes, and book lists from local, state, and federal resources.

Learning Disabilities Association of America (LDA)
4156 Library Rd.
Pittsburgh, PA 15234
(412) 341-1515
Internet: www.ldanatl.org

This nonprofit organization provides resources for parents, teachers, and individuals with learning disabilities through its state and local offices. The LDA hosts an annual conference and publishes books, articles, and videotapes on issues related to learning disabilities.

National Center for Learning Disabilities
381 Park Ave. South, Suite 1420
New York, NY 10016
(212) 545-7510
Internet: www.ncld.org

This nonprofit organization offers parents and educators resources and information on learning disabilities. In addition, it provides referrals to specialists and other professionals who assist individuals with learning disabilities. Advocacy is a primary focus, especially regarding government legislation on behalf of those with learning disabilities. Its annual magazine, *Their World,* holds a wealth of informative articles and an extensive resource list.

Orton Dyslexia Society
Chester Building
8600 LaSalle Rd., Suite 382
Baltimore, MD 21204
(800) 222-3123
Internet: www.pie.org/ods

This international nonprofit association offers advocacy, awareness programs, and information on language programs, research, and publications relating to dyslexia.

Suggestions For Further Reading

Books

Rhoda Cummings and Gary Fisher, *The Survival Guide for Teenagers with LD (Learning Differences)*. Minneapolis: Free Spirit, 1993. Provides information and resources for helping teenagers with learning disabilities succeed in school and how to prepare for adult life.

Kathleen Dwyer, *What Do You Mean, I Have a Learning Disability?* New York: Walker, 1991. This book details the experiences of a child who struggles with a learning disability and eventually gets help; uniquely portrayed through photographs.

Michael Gordon, *Jumpin' Johnny Get Back to Work!* Dewitt, NY: GSI, 1991. Explains what attention deficit hyperactivity disorder is, how it affects a person, and the feelings associated with it.

David Hall, *Living with Learning Disabilities*. Minneapolis: Lerner, 1993. Explains what learning disabilities are and how they impact lives.

Melvin Levine, *Keeping a Head in School*. Cambridge, MA: Educators Publishing Service, 1994. Provides explanations about what learning disabilities are as well as suggestions for compensating or building on strengths to achieve goals.

Cynthia Roby, *When Learning Is Tough: Kids Talk About Their Learning Disabilities*. Morton Grove, IL: Albert Whitman, 1994. Through eight personal stories this book explains how students with learning disabilities feel and cope.

Works Consulted

Books

Bryant J. Cratty and Richard L. Goldman, *Learning Disabilities: Contemporary Viewpoints.* Amsterdam, NY: Harwood Academic, 1996. Although somewhat scientific, this book provides a history of learning disabilities and extensive information on dyslexia and ADD.

Editors of Landmark Outreach Program, *Learning Disabilities: Information and Resources.* Prides Crossing, MA: Landmark Outreach Program, 1996. This book is a collection of articles on issues relating to learning disabilities, including giftedness, ADD, and multisensory teaching methods. Dyslexia and nonverbal learning disabilities are thoroughly discussed.

Lawrence J. Greene, *Learning Disabilities and Your Child: A Survival Handbook.* New York: Ballantine Books, 1987. This book provides information on diagnostic testing and some interesting personal stories that illustrate certain types of learning disabilities. It also includes a glossary with definitions of the different types of learning disabilities and other related terms.

Mary MacCracken, *Turnabout Children: Overcoming Dyslexia and Other Learning Disabilities.* Boston: Little, Brown, 1986. This book reads like a story in that it chronicles the ups and downs of the author's work with various learning-disabled students.

Betty B. Osman, *No One to Play With: The Social Side of Learning Disabilities.* New York: Random House, 1982. This book provides many good examples of the social difficulties children with learning disabilities encounter. It also details how improved academic performance can bolster social skills.

Corinne Smith and Lisa Strick, *Learning Disabilities A to Z: A Parent's Complete Guide to Learning Disabilities from Preschool to Adulthood.* New York: Simon & Schuster, 1997. This book discusses the causes of learning disabilities as well as the diagnostic process. It provides lists of ideas for adapting school or work to meet the needs of people with learning disabilities. It also includes personal stories that illustrate different types of learning disabilities and how people have coped with them.

Sally L. Smith, *Succeeding Against the Odds: How the Learning Disabled Can Realize Their Promise.* New York: Tarcher/Putnam, 1991. Although this book focuses on the experiences of adults with learning disabilities, it integrates this information with childhood experiences in school. It provides a wealth of anecdotes and stories about adults who achieved success in spite of their learning disabilities. It also contains good information on college and the work environment for people with learning disabilities.

Internet Sources

Children and Adults with A.D.D., "What Is Meant by 'Learning Disabilities'?" www.chadd.org/doe/doe_ld.htm. This article offers information on special-education laws pertaining to learning disabilities, statistics on the learning-disabled population, and outlines common characteristics of people with learning disabilities.

Learning Disabilities Association of America, "Through a Child's Eyes," *When Learning Is a Problem.* www.ldanatl.org/pamphlets/learning.shtml.

Saskatchewan Education, "Challenges, Choices, and Changes," January 1998. www.sasked.gov.sk.ca/k/pecs/se/docs/ccc/9801.html. This on-line newsletter provides information about special-education services and resources in Saskatchewan, Canada. This issue includes a brief history of the definition of the term *learning disabilities.*

Periodicals

Gram, "Special Edition—Learning Disabilities and Juvenile Justice," September 1995. This special edition contains articles on the relationship between learning disabilities and juvenile delinquency. It includes statistics, information on how the courts are dealing with offenders who have learning disabilities, and information on reading-instruction methods that have been successful with dyslexic individuals.

Barbara Kantrowitz and Anne Underwood, "Dyslexia and the New Science of Reading," *Newsweek*, November 22, 1999. This article provides information about the most recent scientific brain research in dyslexia, a brief history and description of dyslexia, and the Lindamood-Bell method.

National Institute of Mental Health, press release, "Atypical Brain Activity Detected in People with Dyslexia," July 3, 1996. This press release explains the research findings of a study about how the dyslexic brain works.

———, "Subtle Brain Circuit Abnormalities Confirmed in ADHD," July 14, 1996. This press release provides information about the research findings of a study about what happens in the brains of people with ADHD.

Time, "Cher: Cover Story," March 17, 1975. Although this article is more than twenty years old, it contains some interesting information on Cher's early life as well as quotes about how she coped with childhood problems.

Index

walking-through (technique), 53

Wechsler Intelligence Scale for Children, Third Edition (WISC-III), 38, 60

WISC-III. *See* Wechsler Intelligence Scale for Children, Third Edition

Woodcock Reading Mastery Tests, Revised (WRMT-R NU), 60

word blindness, 11

World Federation of Neurology, 26

writing skills, 17–18, 22, 24

WRMT-R NU. *See* Woodcock Reading Mastery Tests, Revised

Picture Credits

About the Author

Christina M. Girod received her undergraduate degree from the University of California at Santa Barbara. She worked with speech- and language-impaired students and taught elementary school for six years in Denver, Colorado. She has written scores of short biographies as well as organizational and country profiles for educational multimedia materials. The topics she has covered include both historical and current sketches of politicians, humanitarians, environmentalists, and entertainers. She has also written *Native Americans of the Southeast* (Indigenous Peoples of North America series) and *Down Syndrome* (Overview series) for Lucent Books. Girod lives in San Diego, California, with her husband, Jon Pierre, and daughter, Joni.